Sunset

SHEDS
& GARAGES

Detailed Plans and Projects for Your Storage Needs

By Jean Zaputil and Debra Prinzing and the Editors of *Sunset*

Sunset

©2013 by Time Home Entertainment Inc.
135 West 50th Street, New York, NY 10020

ISBN-10: 0-376-01442-3
ISBN-13: 978-0-376-01442-9
Library of Congress Control Number: 2012938009
Fourth Edition. First Printing 2013.
Printed in the United States of America.

OXMOOR HOUSE, INC.
Editorial Director: Leah McLaughlin
Creative Director: Felicity Keane
Brand Manager: Fonda Hitchcock
Managing Editor: Rebecca Benton

TIME HOME ENTERTAINMENT INC.
Publisher: Jim Childs
VP, Strategy & Business Development: Steven Sandonato
Executive Director, Marketing Services: Carol Pittard
Executive Director, Retail & Special Sales: Tom Misfud
Director, Bookazine Development and Marketing: Laura Adam
Executive Publishing Director: Joy Butts
Associate Publishing Director: Megan Pearlman
Finance Director: Glenn Buonocore
Associate General Counsel: Helen Wan

SUNSET PUBLISHING
President: Barb Newton
VP, Editor-in-Chief: Kitty Morgan
Creative Director: Mia Daminato

Sheds and Garages
CONTRIBUTORS
Authors: Jean Zaputil and Debra Prinzing
Managing Editor: Bridget Biscotti Bradley
Art Director: Catherine Jacobes
Production Specialist: Linda M. Bouchard
Photo Editor: Philippine Scali
Photo Coordinator: Danielle Johnson
Project Editor: Sarah H. Doss
Principal Illustrator: Ian Worpole
Senior Imaging Specialist: Kimberley Navabpour
Proofreader: John Edmonds
Indexer: Marjorie Joy
Technical Consultant: Scott Gibson

To order additional publications, call 1-800-765-6400

For more books to enrich your life, visit **oxmoorhouse.com**

Visit Sunset online at **sunset.com**

For the most comprehensive selection of Sunset books, visit **sunsetbooks.com**

For more exciting home and garden ideas, visit **myhomeideas.com**

CONTENTS

GETTING STARTED

Page 6 Great things come in small packages. Adding a shed, garage, or barn to your property will give you lots of functional storage. But don't overlook the aesthetics: Even a diminutive structure can serve as an attractive design element that reflects your home's architecture and enhances the rest of your landscape.

TOOLS and MATERIALS

Page 36 Many factors add up to a successful DIY construction project. Using the right tools and selecting the correct materials are essential. Learn how to streamline the building process with a well-stocked toolbox and high-quality building supplies.

BUILDING BASICS

Page 56 Once you've decided on your project's design, determined the best materials, and gathered your tools, it's time to build. Whether you're exploring new techniques or refreshing skills you already have, this chapter offers everything from basic know-how to advanced ways to finish your shed, garage, or barn.

PROJECTS

Page 96 The projects found in these pages feature specifics for building your shed, garage, or barn. Each one equips you with the fundamentals for planning and constructing a backyard structure that meets your practical storage needs and enhances your outdoor environment.

SIMPLE SPACES

Once relegated to a remote corner of your property where it served only a functional role, the humble shed has finally gained respect as an important piece of architecture in the landscape. Along with other outbuildings—the garage and barn—sheds are now appreciated for their utility and aesthetic qualities.

Whether pint-sized or more ample, sheds, garages, and barns have been elevated to a new role as an exterior design feature. They store, contain, organize, and protect—the traditional purposes for an outdoor structure. But today, a small backyard building can also be a welcoming destination deserving of architectural details like a trellis or deck, and suitable as a focal point in your overall landscape plan. With a few custom details, your project may become a plant-friendly greenhouse, a kid-friendly playhouse, or an adult-friendly garden getaway. Larger structures may serve dual purposes, or be planned with a later conversion in mind so you can use it as a playhouse now and a guest cottage in the future.

Whether you're building, buying, or just browsing, this book covers everything you need to know, from the ground up. Start by considering your many options for style, size, placement, and function. Then survey the tools and materials required to get started and study the overview of basic shed-building techniques—from foundations to finishing details.

Confident weekend warriors can hone their carpentry and construction skills with a small shed project, several of which are featured in Chapter 4. Or you may decide to use these plans as a jumping-off point and experiment with custom details that will personalize your design for a backyard haven that reflects your lifestyle and interests. Chapter 4 also includes large shed projects, garages, and barns for more experienced builders, and for those who merely want to get a sense of the scope of building such a structure but who plan to hire contractors for most of the heavy lifting. We recommend that you always consult with professional contractors when including wiring and plumbing, and whenever you are unsure of how to do some of the more complicated parts of constructing outbuildings, such as framing a roof and pouring a foundation. Many of the projects featured in Chapter 4 can be purchased as kits or complete building plans. See the Resource Guide on page 190 for more information.

Enjoy the process, and soon you'll have your own backyard destination that's both functional and attractive.

GETTING STARTED

Between the back porch and your property's perimeter lies a "middle zone." Certainly, this is where the garden exists, but it's also where a shed, garage, or barn can provide an essential place to store and organize your possessions.

WHAT ARE YOUR OPTIONS?

Fundamentally a simple structure, a shed is highly versatile. It can be a miniature version of your home, or it can be decorated with architectural salvage. Windows, doors, siding, a roof, and interior trim will transform a prosaic storage shed into a cozy, stylish retreat.

FACING PAGE: A basic shed gains charm with many special details, including a metal roof, board-and-batten siding, contrasting window trim, a shelf for displaying flowers and herbs, and attractive exterior lighting.

ABOVE: Hinged carriage doors accommodate a riding lawnmower and other garden equipment (note the useful ramp). Yet with a window box and climbing vines, this functional shed sits comfortably in the heart of the garden.

RIGHT: Today's shed kits are far from bland. This utility shed has modern finishes and cleverly placed clerestory windows just below the metal-trimmed shed-style roof that let in the light while hiding the mess.

FACING PAGE: Think of a garage as a larger, more formal shed. Here, a standard one-car garage mimics house details such as eave depth, roofing, siding, and trim style.

RIGHT: Constructed on a perimeter wall foundation with a concrete slab floor, a garage usually has electricity and may also include plumbing for water and sewage. A second story accommodates storage or a bonus room.

Barns

FACING PAGE: Once basic shelter for animals or crops, barns are now multipurpose structures that house workshops, studios, vehicles, and other equipment. Attractive millwork, a diamond-shaped window, and solid wood doors make this barn an elegant backyard feature.

ABOVE: A large barn can accommodate several uses. Here, the design evokes a classic farm style with red stain, white trim, and an old-fashioned cupola. Inside, there's plenty of space for storing equipment and housing animals.

RIGHT: Strap hinges lend character to rounded double-doors that span a highly functional barn. This structure was framed like a house or shed, but some barns are constructed with traditional pole or timber framing.

TAKING STOCK

What do you want your new structure to do, both now and in the future? Have you always yearned for an art studio? Or do you just need a place to stash garden tools? Think about the best combination of work and storage space for your needs.

FACING PAGE: The selection and placement of two similar prefabricated sheds create an attractive and welcoming destination in the landscape. Walkways that intersect the more naturally planted areas help to visually and physically connect the structures.

ABOVE: Perhaps what you really need are both a potting shed and a greenhouse. Why not combine the two into a single structure that's both useful and charming? Orient the side with clear panels for the amount of sun exposure you want.

RIGHT: This super-efficient utility cupboard fits nicely into the side garden. It has a bonus you might not have considered: a planted roof!

Sometimes the best location is a partially hidden "back" side of a shed or garage. Here, that otherwise blank wall becomes a perfect place for a potting bench, shelves, and tool racks (under the eaves, of course).

A saltbox-style potting shed finds its home under a stand of tall conifers. Useful as your garden headquarters, a shed can double as a personal retreat. A few short steps from the back door and you've made your escape.

THE RIGHT SITE

Your shed's location will determine how useful it is. Function offers some obvious clues: A potting shed should be near the garden, while a private studio may be tucked away from view. Consider weather patterns as well as topography when assessing where to situate the structure.

This sweet garden cottage is ideally placed to lure you there. Walk under the vine-clad arbor, meander along the perennial-edged path, continue by the tall shade tree, and step inside!

Before you commit to a particular location and size for your structure, investigate building codes and zoning restrictions, sun exposure, and seasonal conditions. Also consider how the structure will look from your house or property line.

FACING PAGE: You can't get any closer to the water's edge than this awe-inspiring location. In many areas, building ordinances regulate where you can place your structure and how large it can be. You may choose to limit the size or scope of your project based on minimum square footage requirements for permitting.

ABOVE: Think about access in all four seasons. This carefree cabana, located in an ideal spot for summer, might be less than desirable in winter.

Design Tip: Lay out the perimeter of your proposed shed with stakes and a string line to double-check its proportions.

ABOVE: Zoning restrictions are designed to protect homeowners on both sides of a fence. Common codes govern lot coverage, setbacks, easements, and building height—all considerations when your shed or garage is close to the property line.

LEFT: Consider the views you'll have out the windows and doorways of the structure, as well as the quality of light that streams inside.

FACING PAGE: Siding, roofing, windows, doors, and other finishes will establish your shed's personality. Decide whether it will blend into its surroundings or stand out as an eye-pleasing feature in the landscape.

WHAT'S YOUR STYLE?

Once you have chosen the structure's scale and site, think about its appearance. What style appeals to you, and does it blend with your architecture and the vernacular of your region?

FACING PAGE: The roof of this barn is a classic gable. With traditional shed roofs, the two lean-to additions add contrast and balance and greatly increase its function.

ABOVE: A storybook shed has two dormers built off the central gable roof. Siding painted in a soft green, a red front door, and fan-shaped windows complement the cottage-inspired design.

RIGHT: A saltbox-style shed has a roof that is similar to a gable, but the ridge is offset, providing more headroom at the front of the structure.

LEFT: A gambrel roof is basically a modified gable with two slopes or pitches on each side. Although more complex to frame, it offers significantly more headroom and storage.

BELOW: A lean-to design has a single sloping roof (also called a shed roof). It's inexpensive and easy to frame. This eco-friendly version has a planted roof of drought-tolerant succulents.

FACING PAGE: This symmetrical hip roof is known as a square hip or pyramid style.

ABOVE: You can mimic virtually any architectural style by identifying its trademark features and applying them to your shed. This gable-roofed shed boasts a glassed-in porch with cottage windows and a door.

LEFT: This potting hut has a modified shed roof that allows for an upper row of clerestory windows. The windows bring added light into the interior without sacrificing storage space on the main walls.

FACING PAGE: As formal as can be, this strikingly detailed potting shed is the focal point of this cottage garden. The shingles, cupola, porch, and picket fence define the style, while plantings tie it together with the nearby wicker settee.

CUSTOM TOUCHES

Details large and small make the difference between ordinary and extraordinary. Sheds and garages are themselves pretty basic, but there are endless ways to turn yours into something efficient and attractive.

FACING PAGE: Exterior trim, not to mention the color of paint you choose, can give a diminutive building its strong point of view. Customize your structure with architectural trim and corbels at the roof line, weathered window trim, or rustic doors.

ABOVE: It's the fine points—like trim, siding, a cupola, and a trellis—that changed this garden shed into a classic cottage. The entry arbor supports a wisteria that doubles as a lush, green canopy.

RIGHT: A classic arbor extends the shed's usefulness as a garden feature. Built off an exterior wall, the arbor supports hanging baskets and flowering vines.

LEFT: It's easy to treat green roofs as a fad, but these planted surfaces absorb and filter storm water, cool or insulate the interior space, and return oxygen to the atmosphere. Among its many benefits, an energy-efficient "living roof" can also be beautiful to look at.

FACING PAGE: Wall coverings, flooring, window trim, and other interior finishes transform a basic shed into a little house, complete with a day bed for occasional naps.

FACING PAGE: This barn's gable roof gains stature with an over-sized cupola, or "crow's nest," at its peak. Accessible from inside, the structure features wraparound windows and a small balcony with views of the surrounding landscape and sky.

ABOVE: Put the roof of your shed to work. Depending on its orientation and (ideally) in the absence of over-hanging trees, the roof can support solar panels that reduce your property's energy costs.

Design Tip: Need inspiration? Drive around your community and photograph your favorite architectural styles.

TOOLS and MATERIALS

The construction of a shed, garage, or barn requires the right tools to allow you to work with ease. Choosing the best materials will help ensure a positive outcome. This chapter outlines your choices and gets your shopping list started.

YOUR TOOLS

Having the right tool for the job will make your project go much smoother. As you read this chapter, take stock of what tools you already have and which ones you might want to purchase or rent. Good power tools are becoming more affordable all the time, so if you frequently tackle home improvement projects and find yourself searching for a tool you don't have, now might be the time to make that investment.

Aside from the items listed here, you will need good digging and cutting shovels and a sturdy wheelbarrow when doing foundation work.

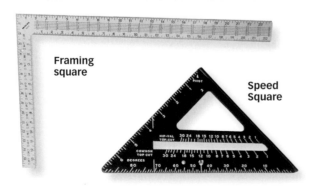

STEEL MEASURING TAPE To measure with precision, make sure you have a heavy-duty locking measuring tape. A 25-foot tape is a good choice for most projects. For longer distances, reel-type tapes are available.

CROSSCUT SAW Even if you have a power saw, a hand-saw is useful for cutting in awkward spots or for cutting notches across the grain of the wood.

SQUARE A Speed Square is used to lay out straight cuts across lumber as well as 45-degree angles. A larger, 16-by-24-inch framing square is useful for laying out roof rafters and checking square over longer distances.

COMPASS SAW Also known as a jab saw, a compass saw lets you make quick cutouts in wood or gypsum wallboard. Since the blade can bend, a model with a replaceable blade is a good choice.

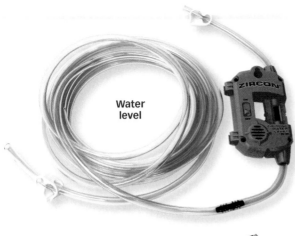

Water level

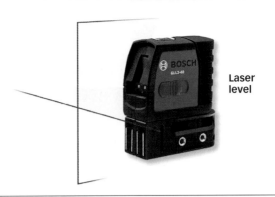

Laser level

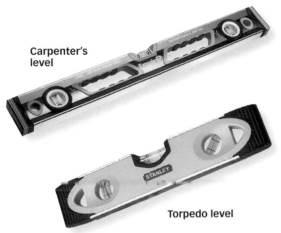

Carpenter's level

Torpedo level

Framing hammer

Finish hammer

ELECTRONIC LEVEL Laser levels have become standard equipment for professionals and vary widely in price and complexity. A basic laser level is affordable for most home-owners and can simplify the building process.

LEVEL Levels are essential for building square structures, and you will probably want several on hand. A standard carpenter's level is 2 feet long. Longer levels, from 4 to 6 feet, are invaluable for large projects. Water levels (essentially water-filled tubes) also measure longer distances with great accuracy. Small torpedo levels are handy in tight spaces.

CLAW HAMMER Use a light curved-claw hammer for finish work and a heavier straight-claw model for framing. Smooth-face hammers minimize dings in the wood, while serrated hammers grip nail heads better. Choose the heaviest hammer you can comfortably wield.

PLUMB BOB Nothing but a pointed weight at the end of a string, a plumb bob uses gravity to transfer overhead points to the ground or floor below.

CHALK LINE This long, spool-wound cord housed within a case of colored chalk is great for marking long cutting lines on sheet materials and laying out reference lines on a wall, ceiling, or floor.

WIRE CUTTERS A pair of 9- or 10-inch lineman's pliers with wire cutters will twist and cut wire and pull out errant fasteners. Locking pliers are another useful tool.

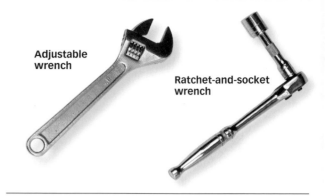

Adjustable wrench

Ratchet-and-socket wrench

WRENCHES An adjustable wrench is good for many bolt or nut sizes but not as precise as an open-end wrench. A ratchet-and-socket set may be required to reach into a countersunk bolt hole.

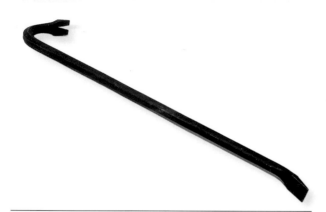

PRY BAR The pry bar is used for demolition and nail removal. It has a claw at one end and an angle at the other that can be driven with a hammer. Larger sizes give more leverage, while smaller ones are better for tight spaces and removing nails.

UTILITY KNIFE Keep one of these handy for cutting and scribing tasks; a retractable, replaceable blade is recommended. The folding type shown is safest, as it opens and closes like a pocketknife.

CLAMPS Clamps hold things where you want them. They're also essential for holding parts together while glue dries. C-clamps are standard, but bar clamps have a longer reach. The spring clamp, which looks like an oversize clothespin, is inexpensive and great for small jobs.

Chisel

Block plane

CHISEL, BLOCK PLANE These basic carpenter's tools are handy for cleaning up saw cuts and joints. The plastic-handled, metal-capped butt chisel can be driven with a hammer. Both planes and chisels are useless unless they're sharp, so you'll want to add a sharpening stone to your tool kit.

Safety Gear

Use common sense and protect yourself during any home improvement project by using safety gear.

- Avoid inhaling harmful vapors, dust, or fibers by using a respirator with a replaceable filter or a dust mask sufficient for sawdust.

- Protect your ears from the noise of power tools by wearing ear protectors. Earmuffs or earplugs will filter noise and still allow you to hear.

- Wear heavy-duty work gloves when handling rough lumber—especially pressure-treated wood. Use rubber or plastic gloves when working with solvents, finishes, or adhesives. Waterproof gloves should be worn in wet conditions.

- Airborne dust and debris require that you wear eye protection. Whether you choose a full-face shield, safety glasses, or safety goggles, make sure they are comfortably fitted, fog-free, and shatterproof.

- You will need protective headgear whenever you're working in tight quarters or with overhead framing members. Save your knees by wearing a pair of knee pads or using a kneeling board.

- Always plug power tools into a GFCI-protected receptacle or extension cord and use shock-resistant, double-insulated tools. Use sound judgment when the weather is bad, and postpone working with power tools if they will be exposed to the elements.

Cordless drill

Hole saw

Star-drive bit

Twist bit

Spade bit

Phillips-head bit

RECIPROCATING SAW Another essential demolition tool, the reciprocating saw is also good for cutting out rough window and door openings. Many blades are available, depending on what you need to cut. For example, a bi-metal blade allows you to cut through metal and rebar easily.

ELECTRIC DRILL AND BITS A ³⁄₈-inch reversible cordless drill is an indespensible tool. Drill bits vary in size and shape according to their use. Holes up to ¹⁄₂ inch in diameter use standard twist bits; carbide-tipped masonry bits will drill through brick, stucco, or mortar; and larger holes require spade bits or a hole saw. To use your drill as a power screwdriver, make sure that it's variable speed. A drill with an adjustable clutch will keep you from "overdriving." A ¹⁄₂-inch drill is used for large-diameter holes or for jobs like mixing joint compound. Some have a hammer drill feature for drilling concrete (used with a special hammer bit). Larger concrete jobs may require a separate hammer drill. A right-angle drill can make working in tight spots easier.

PORTABLE CIRCULAR SAW Quicker than a handsaw, a circular saw with a carbide-tipped combination blade makes both crosscuts and rip cuts. The 7¹⁄₄-inch size is standard. Worm-drive models are generally strongest, and the position of the motor housing allows you to see the cutting line while you cut.

Finish nailer

JIGSAW (SABER SAW) A jigsaw can make both straight and delicately curved cuts. It's a great tool for cutting out brackets and detailed trim. Interior cuts require a drilled pilot hole. Be sure to choose the right blade for your task.

Framing nailer

POWER MITER SAW Also called a "chop saw," the miter saw is the best choice for making precise crosscuts and angled cuts in trim. It cuts framing members to length with precision. A 10-inch miter saw is standard. Compound miter saws cut angles in two directions at once, a feature that may be necessary for rafters or profiled trim. Sliding miter saws can cut stock up to about 12 inches wide.

NAIL GUN Much faster than hammers, nail guns come in many models for a variety of tasks such as roofing, stapling, brads, and flooring. Most nail guns require an air hose and compressor, but newer cordless models are available and run on gas canisters and lithium batteries, giving you more flexibility and less noise. The upfront cost is slightly higher, but the benefits may be worth it.

LUMBER AND HARDWARE

Understanding the basics of how lumber is sized and rated will save you time and money. When you are ordering or buying lumber from a supplier for the first time, it's a good idea to go in person and inspect the material so there will be no surprises. Look ahead to Chapter 3 for basic construction terms.

Lumber Basics

Frame your shed or garage with dimensional lumber. Available in standard sizes, it is primarily softwood sourced from conifers. Spruce-pine-fir (SPF), hem-fir, and Douglas fir are standard. Douglas fir is the strongest of these and may be used for high-stress framing members like floor joists and roof rafters.

Framing lumber is rated for strength. The most common grading system, from best to worst, includes the grades Select Structural, No. 1, No. 2, and No. 3. Lumberyards often sell a mix of grades called No. 2 and Better. Other grading systems used for some lumber (typically 2 by 4s) classify wood according to the grades Construction, Standard, and Utility or as a mixture of grades called Standard or Better. The higher the grade, the more you'll pay. Use the appropriate grade of lumber for each phase of construction.

Building Tip: For strength, choose lumber with a tight grain pattern. The same goes for knots—choose tight over loose.

Pressure-Treated Lumber

Even insect- and moisture-resistant woods like redwood and cedar will rot over time when exposed to water and soil. Pressure-treated wood, made from pine or hem-fir, is treated with chemical preservatives, insecticides, and sometimes water repellants. These woods are cost-effective and durable. Wood that will be in contact with soil must be labeled as "ground contact." Otherwise, above-ground and kiln-dried types are available. Preservatives containing arsenate were once common but have been replaced with less toxic chemicals. As a rule, always wear eye protection, gloves, and a mask when working with pressure-treated lumber, and never burn any scraps. To dispose of treated wood scraps, separate them from nontreated lumber and consult your local solid-waste division for guidelines.

LUMBER	DIMENSIONS
1 by 3	¾ by 2½ inches
1 by 4	¾ by 3½ inches
2 by 4	1½ by 3½ inches
2 by 6	1½ by 5½ inches
2 by 8	1½ by 7¼ inches

If a structure is directly exposed to the elements or in contact with soil, consider pressure-treated lumber (see box on page 44). The heart wood of redwood and cedar, depending on the quality, is naturally resistant to insects and moisture. However, because of cost and strength issues, these woods are typically not used for structural components.

The least expensive lumber available is "green" wood, which is not dried before surfacing and is subject to shrinking, twisting, or splitting. Other lumber is either air dried or kiln dried. Kiln-dried wood is more expensive but can offer the benefits of killing insects, eggs, and fungi in wood, and drying the resin in softwoods. It may also be more stable, but remember that all wood, no matter how it was dried, has the potential for movement and all wood equalizes its moisture content to match the environment. The best way to minimize bows and twists is to start with good lumber stock that's straight and free of large rings and knots.

Douglas fir

Hem-fir

Pressure-treated fir

Pine

Pre-primed pine

Redwood

Plywood
sheathing

Tongue-and-groove
subflooring

Oriented strand
board

Sheathing

Depending on what type of siding your structure will have (see Chapter 3) you may be installing sheathing over your framed walls. Two basic types are available: plywood and oriented strand board (OSB), usually in 4-by-8-foot panels.

Floor sheathing or subflooring has tongue-and-groove edges that interlock and is typically ¾ inch thick but can be as thick as 1⅛ inches. Exterior wall sheathing is usually ½- or ⅝-inch-thick plywood or OSB. Roof decking is most commonly ⅝-inch plywood.

All sheathing should be span rated. The rating looks like a fraction (such as $^{32}/_{16}$), but it isn't. The upper number describes the maximum spacing of supports in inches when the panel is used for roof sheathing, and the lower number denotes the maximum support spacing when the panel is applied as subflooring.

Building Tip: When buying plywood, check that it's rated for wall or roof sheathing.

Post cap	Rafter tie	Joist hanger
Reinforcing straps		Post anchor

Framing Connectors

Many building codes require galvanized metal framing hardware where floor joists meet headers or rim joists, where studs meet sole plates, and so on. Consult your local building code to identify what type of connectors are required in your area.

Even if not required, connectors can add strength and help prevent lumber splits caused by toenailing (see page 72). Connectors handy for shed building include joist hangers, post anchors, angle irons, rafter ties, hurricane ties, and a variety of reinforcing straps. Be sure to attach them with the nails specified by the manufacturer.

Fasteners

Choosing the right fastener is just as important as choosing the right lumber.

NAILS

When joining framing members not exposed to weather, use vinyl- or cement-coated sinkers. These are coated with a dry adhesive and are less likely to work their way out over time. Hot-dipped galvanized or stainless-steel nails are recommended for use with pressure-treated wood or any exposed siding and trim. Use stainless-steel fasteners with cedar to prevent streaking. You can use common or finish nails. Heavy-duty common nails have a head and a thick shank that increases their holding power. Finish nails are used when the head shouldn't show. Drive them nearly flush, then sink the rounded heads with a nail set.

Standard nail sizes are given in "pennies," abbreviated as "d" (from the Latin denarius, a type of Roman coin). The higher the penny number, the longer the nail. Equivalents in inches for the most frequently used nails are shown below.

NAILS AND DIMENSIONS		
3d = 1¼ inches	8d = 2½ inches	4d = 1½ inches
10d = 3 inches	6d = 2 inches	16d = 3½ inches

Choose nails whose length is about three times the thickness of the board being attached. Most shed framing is secured with 8d and 16d nails.

SCREWS

Though more expensive than nails, coated or stainless-steel outdoor screws offer several advantages. Because of their threaded shafts, they have better holding power than nails, they're less likely to be damaged during installation, and they are much easier to remove.

Woodscrews are surprisingly easy to drive into softwoods using an electric drill or screw gun. Other woods require pre-drilled holes equal to the base diameter of the threads. Drywall screws come in smaller sizes than wood screws but are less weather resistant and brittle. The heavy-duty lag screw has a square or hexagonal head and must be tightened with a wrench. Choose screws that measure approximately ⅛ inch less than the combined thickness of the boards you are joining.)

BOLTS

Bolts are heavy-duty fasteners often used as anchors, such as for attaching sole plates to foundations. The machine bolt has a square or hexagonal head, two washers, and a nut. It must be tightened with a wrench at each end. The carriage bolt has a self-anchoring head that digs into the wood as the nut is tightened. Expanding anchors allow you to secure wooden members to a masonry wall or concrete.

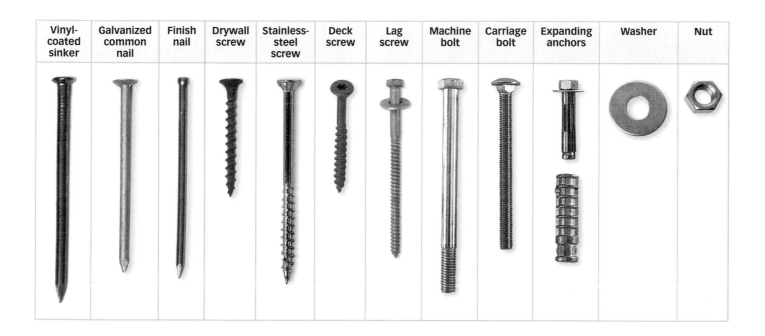

| Vinyl-coated sinker | Galvanized common nail | Finish nail | Drywall screw | Stainless-steel screw | Deck screw | Lag screw | Machine bolt | Carriage bolt | Expanding anchors | Washer | Nut |

ROOFING MATERIALS

Style, durability, cost, and ease of installation all play a part when you are deciding what type of roof to put on your structure. A roof is only as good as its installation, so no matter what type you choose, follow the manufacturer's installation specifications exactly.

WOOD SHINGLES AND SHAKES

Only top-grade shingles and shakes should be used for roofing. Shingles are sawn from chunks of Western red cedar and have a smooth, finished appearance. Shakes are thicker, split on one or both sides, and look more rustic. Manufactured caps are available for hips and ridges. Shingles and shakes are available pre-treated with preservatives or fire retardants, or those substances can be applied during installation. They are more expensive and complicated to install than asphalt shingles but should last 25 to 30 years. Wood roofs may not be allowed in some regions because of flammability, so check your local building and fire codes.

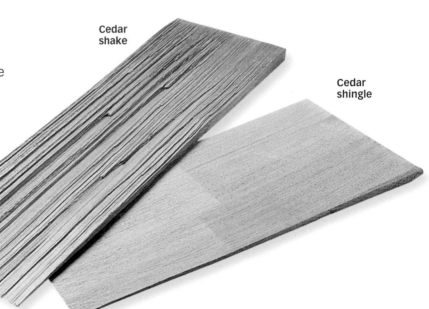

Cedar shake

Cedar shingle

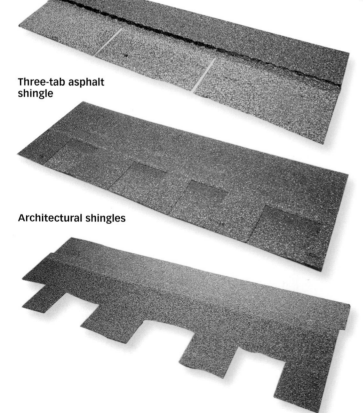

Three-tab asphalt shingle

Architectural shingles

ASPHALT SHINGLES

The most common roofing material, asphalt shingles are inexpensive, easy to install, come with a Class A fire rating, and are available in a wide range of colors and textures. In general, you can expect a shingle roof to last 10 to 30 years, but some can be rated for up to 50 years. They are suitable for any climate but should be used only on roofs with at least a 4-in-12 slope (see page 74). Standard three-tab shingles are a single layer with evenly spaced notches, while architectural shingles are multilayered or laminated for a more dimensional roof.

Building Tip: Make sure that your roofing and flashing materials are compatible.

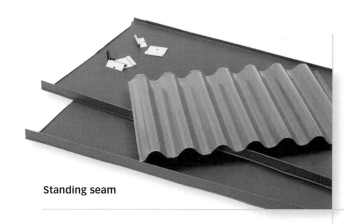

Standing seam

METAL ROOFING

Although the initial cost of a metal roof may be higher, there are many benefits. Metal roofs are easier to install than in the past, and they are typically made of 30 to 60 percent recycled material. They are extremely durable and are resistant to fire and extreme weather conditions. They can last up to 50 years and come in an ever-expanding range of colors, finishes, and textures. Most metal roofing comes with its own edging.

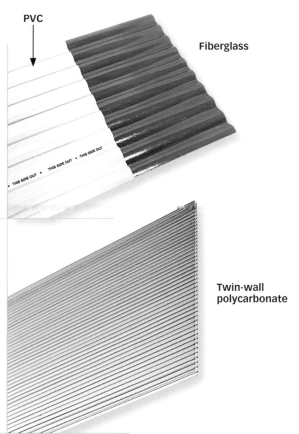

PVC

Fiberglass

Twin-wall polycarbonate

PLASTICS

PVC and fiberglass are old standbys. Acrylic and polycarbonate, available in single- and double-wall panels, are lightweight updates and have the highest light transmission of all plastic glazing. Polycarbonate is also available in triple-wall panels—particularly popular for potting sheds and greenhouses—and in textured and translucent versions. Appropriate roof pitch, structural support, and fasteners are critical for a successful installation. Relatively new to the market are plastic roof tiles, which come in a variety of styles. They are durable and fire resistant, are made from 100 percent recycled material, and meet green building requirements in many areas.

FLASHING

Critical to any roof installation, flashing is used to seal and protect joints from water penetration. It can be made of galvanized sheet metal, aluminum, copper, rubber, or plastic. Metal flashing is available in rolls that you can cut and bend yourself. Typical flashing includes drip edge to cover the ends of eaves and gables; vent collars, which seal the openings around vents; Z-flashing, which seals above windows and doors; and step flashing, used along walls, dormers, and chimneys. To secure the flashing, use fasteners made of the same material. This prevents a chemical reaction that can produce corrosion.

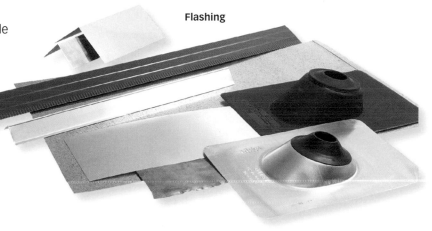

Flashing

SIDING

The outer layer of your walls is as important as the roof for protecting your structure from the elements. More than that, the siding you choose defines the look and style of your building. There are many options for siding materials, including wood, plywood, vinyl, fiber cement, sheet metal, stucco, and brick. Here we focus on the materials most widely used for sheds, garages, and barns.

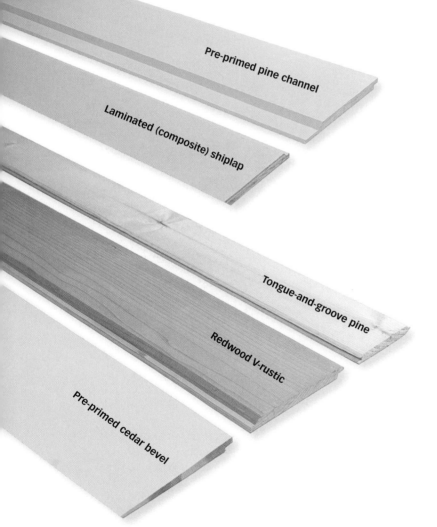

Pre-primed pine channel

Laminated (composite) shiplap

Tongue-and-groove pine

Redwood V-rustic

Pre-primed cedar bevel

PLYWOOD

Exterior-grade plywood siding requires no separate wall sheathing beneath it and remains a popular siding option. Proper installation is critical to prevent moisture damage, and all edges must be sealed before installation. New products are available with pre-sealed or shiplapped edges for easier installation. T1-11 plywood (different from T1-11 OSB) is available with vertical grooves 4 or 8 inches on center and in either sanded or rough finishes. A standard plywood sheet is 4 by 8 feet, though 9- and 10-foot panels can be ordered.

FIBER CEMENT

Made of roughly 90 percent concrete and 10 percent fiberglass, fiber-cement siding is considered a masonry product. It comes in 4-by-8 sheets in smooth or textured finishes as well as shingles, clapboards in several profiles, vertical panels, trim boards, and soffit panels with built-in venting. All types take paint well and are resistant to fire, rot, and insects. These products are also available already primed or painted. Fiber cement is heavy and harder to nail than wood. Cutting with standard tools produces clouds of dust, so use the shears, snap cutters, or specific saw blades recommended by the manufacturer.

Fiber cement

Building Tip: Climate extremes affect the lifespan and maintenance of siding, so choose accordingly.

WOOD SIDING

Sheds and barns often call for traditional board siding or wood shingles (see page 48). Siding boards are typically redwood or cedar, but pine, spruce, and fir are also common. Popular profiles include clapboard or beveled siding, channel, shiplap, V-rustic, and tongue-and-groove. You can also buy square-edge boards and cover the joints between them with narrow battens (see page 83). Tongue-and-groove and shiplap siding can be laid horizontally or vertically. Board texture is either smooth or rough-sawn. Rough-sawn lumber has a texture that accepts stains beautifully.

T1-11 plywood

Exterior Finishes

Add a protective layer to your wood shed with paint, stain, or sealers. Paints and stains can be custom-mixed to any color, or you can select from a wide range of standard colors. Paint companies offer preselected palettes to help coordinate trim and siding, or you may choose to match your home's exterior. Many manufacturers now offer eco-friendly low- and no-VOC products, which are easier on the environment. Here's a closer look at your options:

EXTERIOR PAINT. Both oil- and water-based (latex) paints come in flat, low-luster, semigloss, and high-gloss finishes. Siding is usually painted with a flat finish. Trim and doors often receive low-luster or semigloss for durability. Exterior latex paint is fast-drying and easy to clean up with soap and water. Wood should always be prepared with a coat of primer before the finish coat is applied.

EXTERIOR STAIN. Stains may be semitransparent or solid (opaque). Semitransparent products contain enough pigment to tint the wood surface but not enough to mask the grain, creating an informal or rustic appearance. Solid-color stains are essentially paints. Their heavy pigments cover the wood grain completely, making them suitable

for a formal-looking shed. Under most conditions, semitransparent stain has a shorter life span than either paint or solid-color stain.

WATER SEALER. Applied to unfinished wood, clear sealers won't color the wood but will darken it slightly. You can buy oil- or water-based sealers. Many formulations include both UV blockers and anti-mildew features to protect wood. Some come in slightly tinted versions. Like semitransparent stains, sealers allow you to show off wood with beautiful grain and color, but they do need to be renewed frequently.

WINDOWS AND DOORS

Careful planning and serious shopping are necessary when you're choosing the right windows and doors for your shed, garage, or barn. Consider the architectural style of your structure, light and ventilation requirements, views, and insulating value needed. Be sure to make decisions prior to framing your structure and get manufacturer's specifications for rough opening sizes.

Windows

Windows come in unlimited shapes and sizes. Basic styles—fixed, casement, sliding, awning, or double-hung— are available as standard orders from home improvement centers or window companies. Custom ordering increases the cost. Frames may be wood, wood with vinyl or aluminum cladding, aluminum, vinyl, steel, bronze, or fiberglass. Screens may or may not be included. Wood has the advantage of being paintable in any color or is available primed or factory painted, but cladding, available in a range of colors, eliminates most exterior maintenance problems. Aluminum, the least expensive alternative, is low maintenance but stylistically limited. Vinyl and fiberglass are reasonably priced and virtually maintenance-free but are typically available in only a few colors. Steel and bronze, though more expensive, offer narrow sightlines, strength, and durability.

Vinyl sliding window

Venting skylight

Skylights

Skylights allow extra light and ventilation into interior spaces from above. They're available in standard sizes and shapes, fixed or operable, and with or without screens. They can be made of glass (clear, tinted, translucent, or tempered) or plastic. The frames are typically metal. The structural framing required to support skylights depends on the size and layout. Curbs prevent rain or snow from infiltrating the interior. Consult manufacturer's data for curb, flashing, and installation details.

Doors

Door styles include swinging (traditional), bypass sliding (sliding glass doors), surface sliding (for example, sliding barn doors), or overhead lifted (standard garage doors). Doors may be made of wood with either flush or rail-and-stile panels, metal, or fiberglass, or you may opt for batten doors built on site (see page 84). Options include glass panels and insulation. Steel and fiberglass doors are durable, offer greater fire resistance, and don't expand and contract like wood. Door styles include French doors, patio doors, and Dutch doors. If you're building a simple structure, consider using architectural salvage. Installing wood or metal screen doors adds ventilation. Manufactured pre-hung units include the door, the surrounding jambs, and pre-mounted hinges. You simply place the unit in the framed opening and shim it level and plumb (see page 85). Garage doors come in a variety of styles and finishes from metal and obscure glass combinations to vintage-inspired wood carriage doors (see box).

Pre-hung fiberglass door

Garage Doors

Garage doors, hardware, and openers are available from many sources, but a dealer will be able to supply you with building specifications, price comparisons, style and feature options, and installation. Choose your garage door along with other doors and windows for continuity of design before you start framing. Carefully plan for the size and height of doors, as well as the overhead space required in your building.

Style and finish options have increased greatly in recent years. Wood carriage doors, available in overhead or out-swinging styles, are heavier than other doors and require a more powerful opener. They can be automated (trackless, swing-out openers), as can sliding barn doors. Other wood, aluminum, or steel doors are available in stock designs, semicustom, and custom options. Openers are available with chain, belt drive, and screw type motors and usually include a light source. Keyless entry pads and remote controls add convenience.

INTERIOR TRIM AND INSULATION

Whether or not you finish the interior of your shed, garage, or barn depends on many factors, such as your climate, the function of your building, what you will store there, whether your structure will do double duty (for example, as a garage and a workshop or studio), and the finished appearance. Here are some basic interior options.

Insulation

Fiberglass insulation is inexpensive and offers R-values ranging from R-11 to R-35, depending on thickness. (An R-value rates resistance to heat transfer; the higher the number, the better.) It's available in widths designed to fit between studs and joists spaced 16 or 24 inches apart, as well as in other widths, and with aluminum or paper facing. Rolls or precut lengths fit in standard wall framing. Faced insulation is pressed in place and then stapled onto studs. Some fiberglass products are made with as much as 30 to 40 percent recycled glass and do not contain formaldehyde, which can offgas. Fiberglass will irritate the skin, eyes, and lungs, so wear long pants, a long-sleeved shirt, gloves, goggles, and a respirator when installing it.

Recycled cotton batting, an eco-friendly insulation option, is made primarily from old bluejeans. It's perforated for easier measuring, tearing, and fitting. Recycled plastic bottles are also being made into batt insulation, which is safe to touch and install, compression packed, and available in several R-values.

Extruded polystyrene (rigid foam) insulation is a dense foam board that generally offers about R-5 per inch of thickness. It's inexpensive, comes in 4-by-8-foot sheets, and is available pre-scored for commonly used widths. Sheets may have tongue-and-groove edges so they can be joined to create a continuous layer. Often used as a backer for vinyl siding, rigid foam insulation is waterproof and can be used above or below ground. Insect infestation can be a problem in certain regions, especially if the insulation is in contact with soil.

Cellulose loose fill is commonly made from 75 percent recycled paper combined with a flame retardant. Its R-value is similar to that of fiberglass—about R-3.2 per inch of thickness. Loose fill can be blown in and is an option for ceilings with low clearances. Specially treated cellulose, combined with a binder, can be sprayed between framing studs, providing added soundproofing and a full R-value. Check installation requirements carefully. Even though it has none of the irritating properties of fiberglass, you should use safety equipment to protect your skin and eyes.

Fiberglass

Recycled cotton

Rigid foam

Cellulose

Wall Coverings

Interior walls can be left bare or covered. If you've added insulation, it's best to cover the walls to prevent damage to the insulation over time. Think carefully about storage needs before sheathing interior walls. You may want to build the framework for storage components into the structure of your shed first. No matter what material you choose, all building inspections should be completed before you finish the walls. Gypsum wallboard (drywall) is an economical and easy-to-install wall covering; use $\frac{1}{2}$- or $\frac{5}{8}$-inch sheets. Plywood siding (see page 50), though more expensive than drywall, holds up well in garages and sheds. If your building will function as a work or studio space, consider upgrading to solid wood paneling. It's available in many colors and patterns and installs easily with construction adhesive and/or nails. Fiber-cement board, sheet metal, or architectural salvage could be used as well, or in combination with other materials for an interesting and functional interior.

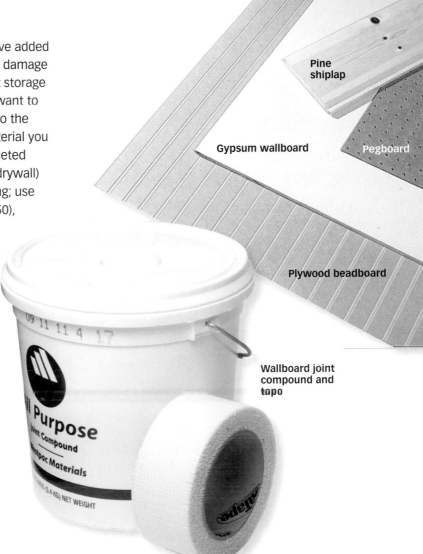

Pine shiplap

Gypsum wallboard

Pegboard

Plywood beadboard

Wallboard joint compound and tape

Moldings

Moldings and Trim

Stock moldings are available at lumberyards or home centers either unfinished or primed. Another option is to combine stock lumber and moldings to create your own trim pieces. Paint-grade pine moldings have visible finger joints along their length and are less expensive than stain-grade oak or other hardwoods. Moldings made from medium-density fiberboard (MDF) are usually primed, less expensive than wood, and take paint very well. They may not be durable enough for areas like workshops and do not hold up well in damp conditions, so consider PVC or fiber-cement moldings.

BUILDING BASICS

Whether you're exploring new techniques or refreshing skills you already have, this chapter offers the essential construction know-how for building your shed, garage, or barn. You'll also find information on adding water and electricity and finishing the interior.

PREPARING TO BUILD

By now you have a pretty clear idea of the type of structure you're building. You've considered the site, weather, soil conditions, and drainage needs. You know the function of the building and therefore its size and storage requirements. You've determined accessibility—not just for you but for installing electrical and plumbing systems—and even have some ideas about architectural style.

Whether you've decided to purchase a kit or a set of plans, or design and build it yourself from the ground up, make sure that your structure is built to code. Small sheds may not require a permit; accessory structures smaller than a certain square footage (usually 100 to 200 square feet) are often exempt. Permits are usually required for garages and barns. Check with your local building department to find out what the permit requirements are and what inspections will be required. Don't break ground until you have a final permit in hand and have met any pre-construction requirements. Always have your utilities located prior to digging.

Start the project with a realistic look at your own skills and think about whether you need some construction help. If your building is large, you will need at least one extra set of hands to set roof trusses, rafters, and joists in place, and to raise walls. Hiring a professional to install parts of your project can be a smart decision and save time and money in the end. This chapter outlines the essential construction elements of sheds, garages, and barns. See Chapter 4 for step-by-step projects.

Shed Kits

If you want a new shed but would rather not build one from scratch, consider a shed kit (see page 190 for a list of kit manufacturers). There are two basic types of kits available: parts kits and prefabricated kits. Parts kits supply you with a set of plans and most (if not all) of the materials. You then cut the pieces to size and assemble the shed. Prefabricated kits arrive partially constructed for on-site assembly to form the floor, walls, and roof. Most kit manufacturers offer an assembly service and can dispatch a crew to put the shed together for you.

Manufacturers may offer custom design options, or add your own paint, trim, windows, skylights, arbor, or an adjacent patio or deck to turn a simple shed kit into the focal point of your yard.

Anatomy of a Shed

Like a house, a shed has a foundation, floor, walls, roof, siding, windows, doors, and trim. The foundation can be as temporary as skids (shown below) or more substantial piers, poured footings, or a concrete slab (shown at right). While concrete slabs can double as floors, other foundations require floor platforms made from evenly spaced joists and structural sheathing. "Stick-framed" walls are built in sections from 2-by lumber. They are secured to the floor or perimeter wall foundation and tied together with double top plates above. Rafters run between the top plates and a central ridge board and are sheathed in preparation for the roofing material. Roofing felt is installed over the sheathing. Rough openings are carefully framed to accept windows and doors, and the exterior walls are covered with sheathing and/or siding. Interior and exterior finishes and trim are added to complete the project. The above steps are covered in order in the following sections, beginning on page 62.

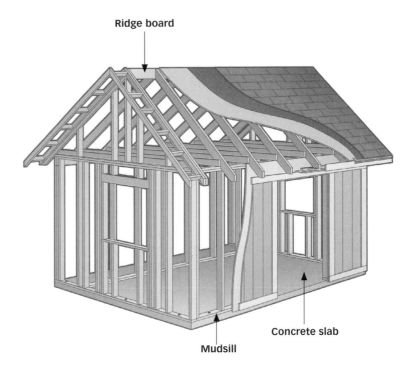

Ridge board

Mudsill

Concrete slab

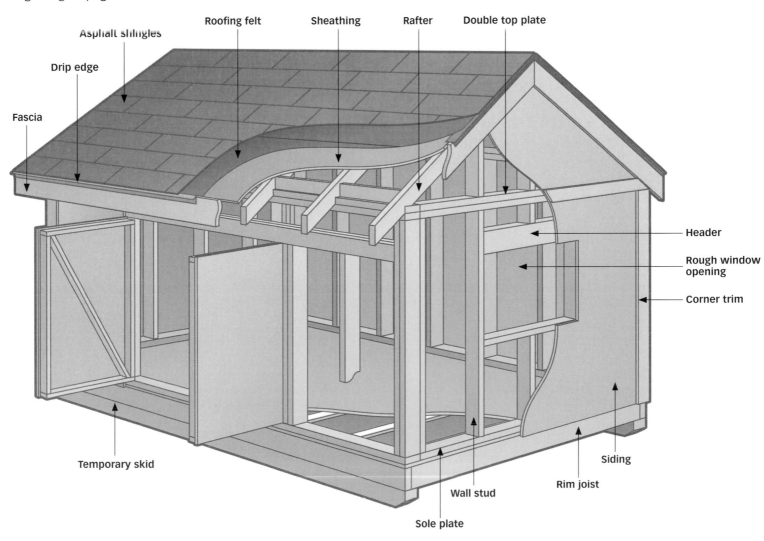

Asphalt shingles

Roofing felt

Sheathing

Rafter

Double top plate

Drip edge

Fascia

Header

Rough window opening

Corner trim

Temporary skid

Wall stud

Sole plate

Rim joist

Siding

Anatomy of a Garage

Depending on where you live, a garage foundation may be a concrete slab. Be sure to check with your building department, as your region may require a perimeter wall foundation that extends below the frost line (see page 63). Depending on the complexity of your project, plumbing and electrical hookups, as well as sill anchors, will need to be in place (see pages 88–89 for information on systems). Walls are typically built in sections and raised one at a time. By temporarily bracing the walls, you can secure the bottom sill to the foundation with concrete anchors. Other straps and anchors may be required for wind and seismic loads. Be sure to follow the manufacturer's installation instructions carefully for the required hardware.

Rough openings are framed for doors and windows with headers at the top to support the weight of the roof. You'll need to have properly engineered header beams to frame large openings like garage doors. Ceiling joists span the top plates of the walls, and rafters are attached to the top plate and to the ridge board to form the roof. Framing for skylights or any plastic panels should be completed at this time. Rafters are covered with sheathing and roofing felt, then finished with shingles, shakes, or metal roofing. Windows and doors are installed, then exterior sheathing and/or siding and trim are added. Plumbing and electrical systems are installed before any optional interior finishes are applied.

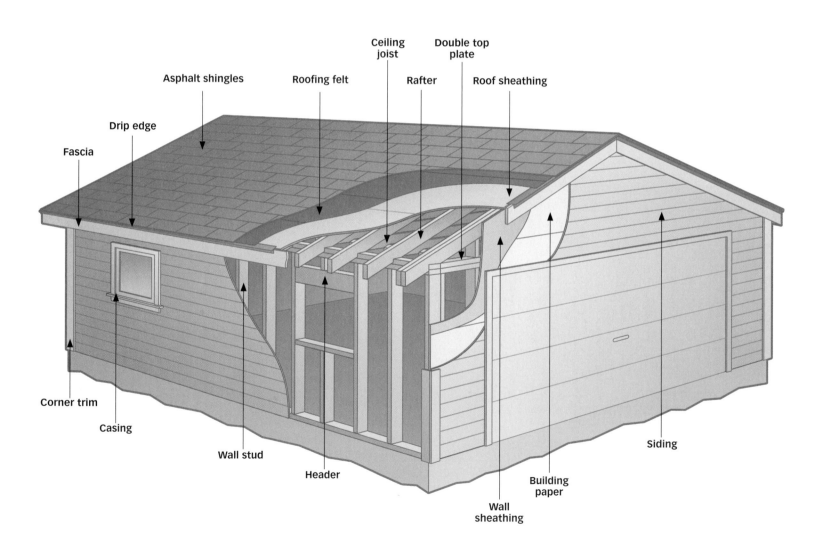

Ceiling joist

Double top plate

Asphalt shingles

Roofing felt

Rafter

Roof sheathing

Drip edge

Fascia

Corner trim

Casing

Wall stud

Header

Wall sheathing

Building paper

Siding

Barn Basics

Because barns are often larger than garages or even houses, alternative techniques are used for their construction. Stick framing, pole construction, and timber framing are the most common.

Stick-framed barns are usually built on a slab foundation. Barn roofs are often built with premade trusses (see page 75). The gambrel-style roof shown at right is a popular choice for barns and offers maximum storage space above.

A pole barn, or post-frame construction, (shown below) is quicker to build and less expensive because there are no perimeter footings and less site work is necessary. Poles, either round or square, are driven directly into the ground or set into piers. Horizontal boards called girts join the poles. Vertical siding is then applied to enclose the space. Roof framing is simple, as rafters are run between the uppermost wall girts and the ridge girt. Many engineering calculations are required to determine the sizing, spacing, and installation depth of posts. Posts driven directly into the ground should be pressure treated.

A timber-framed barn will last a lifetime or longer. It is built with large, heavy timbers and age-old techniques such as mortise-and-tenon joinery. Timbers can span great distances and eliminate the need for wall studs. Timber framing is not a project for a novice, but a highly skilled builder, and should not be attempted by anyone without training (there are a number of timber-framing schools nationwide).

Barn doors may be sliding or overhead, and either style can be opened manually or automatically. Height and size requirements, durability, function, cost, and weight should all be considered when you are choosing what type of barn doors to install.

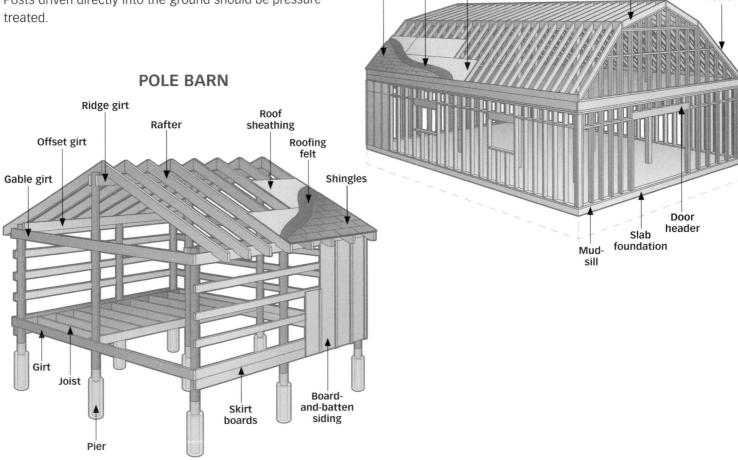

POLE BARN

Ridge girt · Offset girt · Gable girt · Rafter · Roof sheathing · Roofing felt · Shingles · Girt · Joist · Skirt boards · Board-and-batten siding · Pier

STICK-FRAMED GAMBREL BARN

Asphalt shingles · Roofing felt · Roof sheathing · Ridge board · Upper rafter · Lower rafter · Door header · Slab foundation · Mud-sill

FOUNDATIONS

The basis for any building is a solid, level, and square foundation. Foundations must be installed on undisturbed, bearing soil. If soil has been disturbed, replace it with compacted crushed rock for stability.

Small sheds can be built with a pair of skids or precast concrete piers as a foundation (see below). Larger sheds require a more permanent foundation with the structure attached to the concrete slab and/or footing. Garages and some barns are best built on slab or perimeter wall foundations (see page 63).

Many shed foundations can be installed successfully by the average homeowner, but a slab or perimeter wall foundation, especially for larger buildings, may call for professional help and require large footings, building forms for poured concrete, reinforcing steel (rebar), and a mixer for the delivery of loads of concrete.

Temporary Foundations

A skid foundation is the easiest to build. The skids allow you to move the shed to a different location and also classify it as a non-permanent structure per many building codes. Skids are made of pressure-treated 4 by 6s with tapered ends. Provide ample drainage by excavating 4 to 5 inches of soil where the shed will be. Then install 4 to 5 inches of compacted crushed rock. Good drainage and subgrade decrease soil erosion and stabilize the shed.

Precast concrete piers or blocks (like those shown below) have notches in their tops to accept dimensional lumber and can be used to make a temporary foundation.

A pier foundation needs adequate drainage for stability. Excavate the entire shed area (to avoid grass growing under your shed), or just the area of the pier blocks, and fill with compacted crushed rock to a depth of 4 to 5 inches.

For either type of temporary foundation, the floor frame is built with 2-by joists and covered with exterior-grade plywood. For details, see pages 68–69.

SKID FOUNDATION

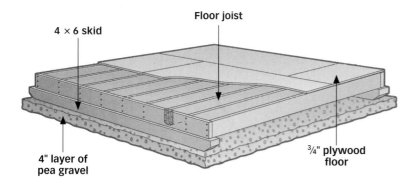

4 × 6 skid

Floor joist

4" layer of pea gravel

¾" plywood floor

PRECAST PIERS

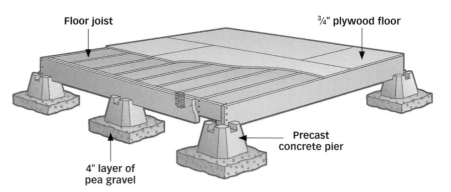

Floor joist

¾" plywood floor

Precast concrete pier

4" layer of pea gravel

Permanent Foundations

Poured footings, slabs, and perimeter wall foundations are all types of permanent foundations. Slabs are used primarily in warm climates where no frost action occurs. Perimeter walls allow the footing portion to be placed below the frost line to reduce heaving and cracking. Both types of foundation are reinforced with rebar and/or wire mesh.

A poured footing, with the base below the frost line, is the simplest permanent foundation and is well suited for small structures like sheds. Concrete tube forms or hand-built forms are used to shape the footings. The structure attaches to the footings with ½-inch anchor bolts and/or metal post bases embedded in the wet concrete. Make sure that the tops of the footings are set high enough out of the soil so that moisture will not wick into the wood structure.

An on-grade slab foundation is made of a minimum of 4 inches of concrete poured on a bed of crushed rock and reinforced with wire mesh. A thickened edge, extending a minimum of 12 inches below the soil level, runs along the perimeter and is reinforced with rebar.

If you live in a cold climate, your building code may require a perimeter wall foundation consisting of a footing that extends below the frost line and foundation walls built over that footing. The footing portion of the wall is typically equal in depth to the width of the wall and twice as wide, but your code will spell out exact dimensions. The footing and wall sections are typically poured independent of one another and connected by rebar set into the footing at the time of the pour. Forms are stripped after the concrete is cured. A reinforced concrete slab floor can be poured between perimeter walls.

POURED FOOTING

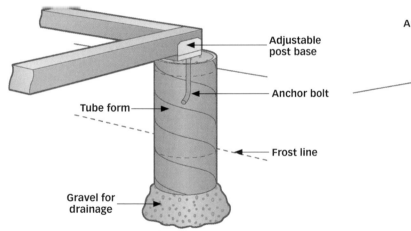

- Adjustable post base
- Anchor bolt
- Tube form
- Frost line
- Gravel for drainage

ON-GRADE SLAB

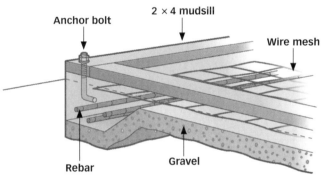

- Anchor bolt
- 2 × 4 mudsill
- Wire mesh
- Rebar
- Gravel

PERIMETER WALL FOUNDATION

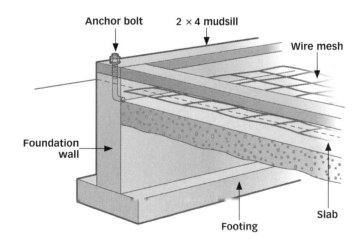

- Anchor bolt
- 2 × 4 mudsill
- Wire mesh
- Foundation wall
- Slab
- Footing

Installing a Temporary Foundation

Easy to install, this simple foundation substitutes solid concrete blocks (4 by 8 by 16 inches) for precast piers. The blocks are installed on beds of compacted crushed rock. A temporary foundation like this one works best as a base for a small shed, playhouse, lean-to storage unit, or other structure that you might want to move one day.

1 DIG THE HOLES Lay out your foundation as detailed on page 66. Arrange blocks in rough position according to your plan and spade around them to mark their locations. Remove the blocks and dig a hole about 4 inches deep in each footing location. If you don't want anything growing under the shed, remove the vegetation between blocks and fill in with gravel.

2 PLACE AND LEVEL BLOCKS Fill each hole with crushed rock and tamp it down with a hand tamper or a wood block. Reposition the corner blocks and check your layout by measuring diagonally from corner to corner; when the measurements match, the layout is square. Next, check each block for level in both directions and use a small sledgehammer or mallet to tap them into alignment. Don't worry about whether they're level with one another at this point.

3 LEVEL THE ROWS Place a long, straight 2 by 4 from one end block to the other and lay a level on top. Add or remove gravel as needed and re-tamp each end block to level it. When the ends are level with one another, level the intermediate blocks. Continue with the same technique, leveling each additional row to the end block of the previous row. When you're finished, recheck the level overall and the diagonal measurements to make sure the foundation is square.

Installing Permanent Footings

Before you start to dig, be sure to mark the location of possible utilities. Holes for poured footings can be dug with a posthole digger. Though heavier, a power auger (shown below) will be quicker. Most rental centers carry these—when you rent one, have the salesperson explain its operation. If you have many bags of concrete to mix, you can also rent a portable gas or electric mixer, which will save time and effort.

1 DIG THE HOLES Lay out your foundation with batter boards and mason's line, as described on page 66. Your local code will specify how deep the frost line is and how far below it you need to dig. In most cases, the code will require you to provide drainage by adding a layer of gravel below the footings. If using concrete tube forms, make sure they extend at least 2 inches above the finished soil grade.

2 MIX AND POUR CONCRETE Pour premixed concrete into a wheelbarrow and make a depression in the center. Add the recommended amount of clean water and mix using a mortar hoe or shovel, moving the concrete back and forth until all the water is absorbed by the mix. Insert a concrete form (Sonotube or equivalent) in the hole, then slowly shovel in the concrete. Air bubbles trapped in concrete can weaken it, so use a thin scrap of wood to poke the concrete and release any trapped air. Draw a 2 by 4 over the top of the form to level, or screed, the concrete.

3 INSTALL ANCHORS Reposition the mason's lines on the batter boards so that they cross the center of the footing. Then use a plumb bob to mark the anchor location. Push each anchor into the wet concrete, wiggling it to allow concrete to fill in the gaps. Adjust its position so the anchor is centered and use a torpedo level to check that the anchor is level and plumb.

Pouring a Slab Foundation

The on-grade slab foundation shown here is designed for a relatively small building and a mild climate. Even though small slabs are fairly easy to install, you'll need a helper for leveling. Be sure to follow all building codes for your area and set the top of the slab far enough above the natural grade to keep moisture from wicking into the structure. Typically, building codes require a minimum of 6 inches between the soil and the siding. As a reminder, larger foundations are best installed by professionals, as they may require deep footings, extensive formwork, reinforcement, and several loads from a concrete mixer.

1 LAY OUT THE FOUNDATION Look over your shed plan and roughly lay out the corners of the footings with temporary stakes. Position pairs of batter boards (2-by-4 stakes driven into the ground and spanned with 1 by 4s) forming right angles about 18 inches behind each corner. Stretch mason's line between batter boards and use a 3-4-5 triangle (see page 67) to check for 90-degree corners. Secure the lines as shown with nails driven into the batter boards.

2 DIG FOOTINGS For a slab like this one, dig a 12-to-16-inch-deep trench along the perimeter for a 12-inch-wide footing (see page 63). Excavate a minimum of 4 to 5 inches of soil from the rest of the slab area and install 4 to 5 inches of compacted crushed rock. If the mason's lines are in your way, temporarily loosen them while you dig.

3 BUILD FORMS

Forms for slab foundations are built from 2-by boards held in place with stakes. Rebar and wire mesh should be added before you pour. Here, #5 rebar is placed on bricks in the bottom of the perimeter trench to elevate it and allow concrete to encase it. A 6-mil vapor barrier can be laid over the gravel slab section and #10 reinforcing mesh placed on top, inset 2 inches from the forms. The mesh should be elevated (thinner, paving bricks work well) but still be in the bottom half of the slab.

4 POUR CONCRETE

For a slab foundation, the concrete mixer will arrive with a load of concrete and the crew will quickly pour it into the form. Use a screed—typically a long, straight 2 by 4 or 2 by 6—to level the surface. Drag the screed with a sawing motion back and forth along the top of the form, then carefully smooth the concrete with a bull float.

5 INSTALL ANCHORS

Attach the walls to the slab using ½-inch anchors set into the concrete. For maximum holding power, these are typically shaped like a J. To lay out anchor locations, snap a chalk line to mark the center of the bottom sills and then measure and mark anchor locations per your plans. Push each anchor into the wet concrete and wiggle it, allowing the concrete to completely encase the anchor. Mist the slab with water and cover it with a layer of plastic. Keep the surface moist for two to three days.

3-4-5 Triangle

One of the oldest and most reliable ways to check a corner for 90 degrees, or square, is to use a 3-4-5 triangle. To do this, measure one line and mark a point 3 feet from the corner. Next, measure and mark the other line 4 feet from the same corner. Measure the hypotenuse, or diagonal, between the 3-foot mark and the 4-foot mark with a tape measure. If the lines are perpendicular, the distance will measure exactly 5 feet. If it doesn't, you'll need to adjust the position of one of the lines to achieve 90 degrees.

FLOOR FRAMING

A concrete slab on grade typically acts as the floor of a shed, garage, or barn as well. But for structures built on temporary skids or piers, or some buildings with permanent footings, your plan may call for a wood-framed floor. The key to floor framing is to start with straight, parallel beams or rim joists mounted to the foundation. Check local building codes for the size of floor joists needed and mount them between the rim joists 12 to 24 inches on center, or as specified. The floor frame is covered with sheathing or subflooring (see page 46), usually ¾-inch tongue-and-groove plywood or OSB (oriented strand board).

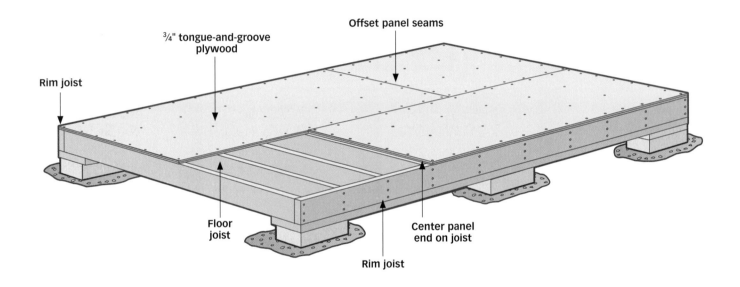

¾" tongue-and-groove plywood

Offset panel seams

Rim joist

Floor joist

Center panel end on joist

Rim joist

Cut It Straight

One of the best ways to ensure accuracy when you are framing floors, walls, or a roof is to make precise, straight cuts. For safety, support long pieces of lumber on both sides of the cut. Use sawhorses and allow space for scraps to fall away. For repeat cuts, make simple jigs to mark lumber quickly and accurately.

A Speed Square can help guide cuts with a circular saw, as shown at right. Place it on the wood being sawn, with the lip against the edge. Position the saw against the square with the blade on the waste side of the marked line. Hold the square firmly in place as you push the saw through the cut, keeping the saw base in constant contact with the square.

Building a Platform Floor

Now is the time to indulge your inner perfectionist. When you are framing a floor, the parts should be cut and assembled as precisely as possible. Any imperfections will cause trouble later as you try to square the structure's walls and roof.

1 INSTALL RIM JOISTS

Cut a pair of straight rim joists to sit atop the foundation. In this example, pressure-treated rim joists are nailed to 2-by-8 mudsills, which span the evenly spaced concrete blocks below (see page 62). Per some building codes, you may be required to lock joists or sills in place with steel ground anchors.

2 MARK JOIST LOCATIONS

Lay out joist spacing 12 to 24 inches on center (or as specified) along the rim joists. If your final joist space is larger than the others, add an extra joist to ensure adequate support.

3 INSTALL JOISTS

Cut floor joists to length. Position them between the rim joists (be sure they're not twisted) and fasten them using either 3-inch outdoor screws or 16d galvanized nails driven through each rim joist into the joist ends. Galvanized joist hangers may also be used (see page 46).

4 ADD THE SUBFLOOR

Lay a full sheet of ¾-inch tongue-and-groove plywood or OSB across the joists flush with the edges. Trim ends as necessary to center any seams on joists. Tack the panel in place with 2-inch deck screws or 8d nails (for firmer flooring, first apply a bead of construction adhesive to the joists), but don't screw or nail along the leading edge just yet.

Start the next row as shown with a half sheet to offset the seams, then finish adding plywood. Go back and add fasteners every 6 inches along the perimeter and 12 inches elsewhere.

WALLS

With the foundation and floor in place, you can start to frame the walls of your building. A typical wood frame wall consists of continuous, vertical 2-by-4 wall studs spaced 16 or 24 inches on center. These span the bottom, or sole, plate (attached to the subfloor) and a top plate, which is later doubled when the walls are positioned. On slab foundations, the sole plate is called a mudsill and should be made of pressure-treated wood.

To frame an opening for a window or door, a horizontal framing member called a header is installed to assume the load of the wall studs that were removed. The header's size varies according to the distance spanned and the load carried, but most are made from two 2-by members on edge with a ½-inch plywood spacer between them—which adds up to 3½ inches, the thickness of a 2-by-4 wall. They may also be cut from a larger beam.

The header is supported by trimmer studs (also called jack studs), which are attached to the inside face of full-length studs known as king studs. The shorter pieces that run between the header and the top plate or from the underside of a rough sill to the sole plate or mudsill are called cripple studs.

In most cases, the rough opening for a window or door should be ½ to ¾ inch wider and taller than the unit you're installing, but always consult the manufacturer's guidelines for the rough opening size. The extra space lets you adjust the unit for level and plumb.

WALL FRAMING

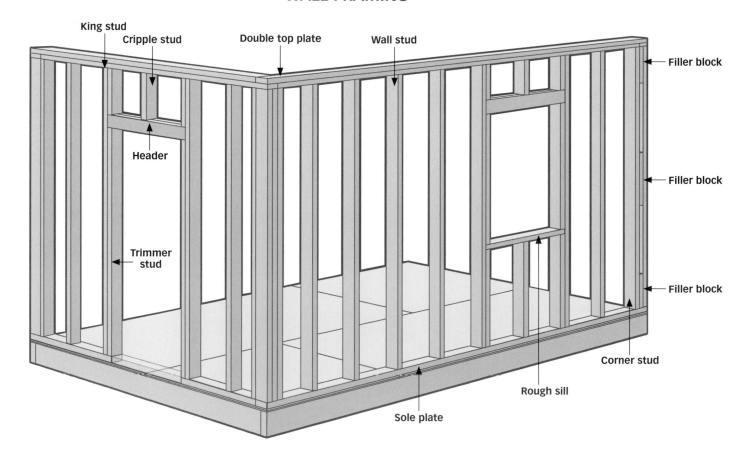

King stud · Cripple stud · Double top plate · Wall stud · Filler block · Header · Filler block · Trimmer stud · Filler block · Corner stud · Rough sill · Sole plate

Assembling a Wall

Before starting, check and recheck your plans for overall wall heights and confirm rough openings for windows and doors. When building walls, work on a level surface that is clean and free of debris to help you keep the walls flush.

1 MARK THE PLATES

To make sure that wall studs align, mark their locations on the top and bottom plates for each wall individually. Choosing straight lumber is critical; double-check your measurements and cut carefully. Align the top and bottom plates when marking or, if you prefer, clamp or screw them together temporarily. Set the plates on edge and, measuring from one end, make a mark at 1½ inches and another at 15¼ inches (for 16-inch-on-center spacing) or 23¼ inches (for 24-inch-on-center spacing). A 1½-inch-wide framing square allows you to mark the edges of each stud. Continue to measure and mark a line every 16 or 24 inches to indicate stud placement.

2 ATTACH WALL STUDS

Now separate the top and bottom plates. (On a slab foundation, position the mudsill on the slab and transfer the anchor locations onto it; drill slightly oversize holes for the anchors to pass through.) Cut sufficient studs to length for the wall, and end-nail them as shown to the top and bottom plates with 16d nails. Align the studs with the marks you made on the plates. For nailing tips, see page 72.

3 FRAME ROUGH OPENINGS

Cut and assemble correctly sized headers for doors and windows (per local building codes). Also cut king, trimmer, and cripple studs and rough sills per your plan. Cut trimmers to the height of the rough openings and then attach them to king studs before installing them. Place each header on top of the trimmers and fasten it to the trimmer and king studs. Install cripple studs above headers and below sills.

continued »

Nailing It

The key to successfully driving a large nail is to start with small hammer taps, then progress to looser, fuller swings, hitting the nail square. Toenailing (below) requires you to drive the nail at about a 30-degree angle. For a novice, it's sometimes easiest to drill a small pilot hole before nailing. If you'd rather not toenail, try screws instead, or consider using metal framing connectors (see page 46).

Siding and trim jobs often call for finish nails. To avoid hammer dings, drive each nail until it's about ⅛ inch above the wood, then tap its head below the surface with a hammer and nailset.

4 RAISE THE WALL

Get help if you need it and lift the wall so its top plate is about waist high. Align the outside edge of the bottom plate with the outside edge of the floor or slab. Raise the wall upright by "walking" your hands down the studs. (On a slab foundation, make sure all the anchors pass through the mudsill.)

5 BRACE THE WALL

As you lift each wall section into place, keep it upright by using a 1-by-4 brace at each end. Nail the far end of each brace to a stake driven into the ground. Use a level and recheck the wall section for plumb. While holding the wall in place, have a helper nail or screw the brace to the wall section. Now recheck the wall for plumb again and make adjustments as necessary. For larger walls, you may need significantly more bracing.

Add Siding Now?

For a small structure like a shed, wall sheathing and/or siding is sometimes more easily installed while the wall is flat on the ground. If this is your choice, be sure the wall is square and attach the siding as described on pages 80–83. Be aware that walls are significantly heavier with the siding attached.

6 SECURE THE WALLS

Before securing the walls, measure diagonals inside the structure and adjust for square. Also check the walls for level and shim if needed. Attach each wall section to the slab or floor. For a slab foundation, place washers over the anchor bolts and thread on nuts. For wood floors, drive nails or screws every 16 inches or so through the sole plate and into the floor. The fasteners should penetrate about halfway into the floor joists or rim joists. Avoid framed door openings, as they will be cut away.

The corners where two walls meet will require extra framing. Add 2-by-4 filler blocks against the end stud and then install an extra corner stud. By creating a corner "post," you can start at one end and nail the walls together with 16d nails. Recheck for level and plumb in case the walls may have shifted slightly. Remove the temporary wood braces.

7 DOUBLE THE TOP PLATE

After the walls are in place, a second plate, or double top plate, is added to create a more rigid structure that will support the roof. Cut the double top plates to lengths that overlap the first top plates' joints. Secure the double top plates to the top plates with 8d nails every 16 inches. Drive in two nails at the ends of the plates that overlap intersecting walls. Use a handsaw or a reciprocating saw to remove the bottom plate from door openings.

ROOFING

Most shed, garage, or barn roofs are variations on the simple gable roof. Evenly spaced rafters run from the top plates of the walls up to the ridge board. A roof overhang often extends past the walls. The ends of the rafters are often covered with trim called fascia.

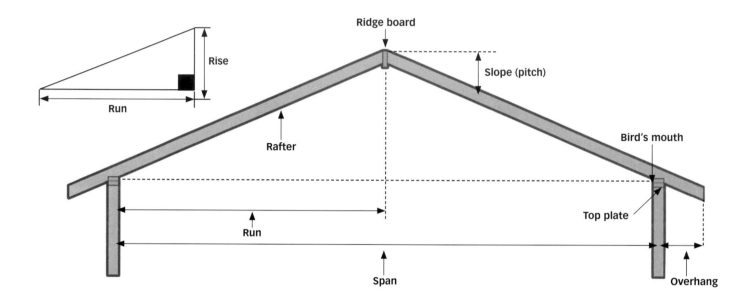

Roofs must be designed to carry dead loads (from the structure itself, roofing, ceiling, insulation, etc.), live loads (from rain, snow, and ice—or you, if you're on the roof), and wind loads, both lateral and vertical. Rafter size varies depending on the size of the structure and the load it will be carrying, from 2 by 4s for a small shed to 2 by 10s or larger for garages and barns. Typical spacing ranges from 12 to 24 inches on center. (Check your building code for rafter dimensions and spacing requirements.) The ridge board is usually one size larger than the rafters (for example, a 2-by-8 ridge board for 2-by-6 rafters).

The slope, or pitch, of a roof is defined as a rafter's vertical rise in inches per 12 inches of horizontal run. For example, a rafter that rises 5 inches for every 12 inches of run has a 5:12 or 5-in-12 slope. Roofs with steeper slopes require longer rafters, provide easy runoff for rain and snow, and offer the potential for usable interior space. Asphalt roofs require a minimum of a 4:12 slope. Shed roofs vary from 3:12 to 12:12. Steep shed roofs allow for additional light or ventilation on the ridge side.

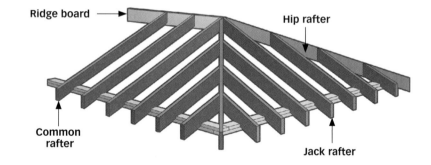

Hip Framing

Framing a hip roof can be a challenge. Multiple angled rafter cuts make it one of the most complicated options for roof framing. Understanding the specialized names of the parts is essential. Common rafters (blue in the drawing) run the full distance from the ridge board (shown as yellow) to the double top plates. Hip rafters (green) connect to the ridge at an angle where the two planes of the roof meet. Jack rafters (shown as red) run from the hip rafters to the plates.

Joists or No Joists?

Ceiling joists are horizontal framing members that span the top plates of the structure and prevent the roof load from forcing the walls apart. Small sheds don't necessarily require joists, but larger sheds and garages probably will. As with rafters, the size of the joists depends on the size of the structure, so check your local building code. Typical joist spacing is 16 or 24 inches on center. Collar beams or ties are sometimes required for buildings that are not large enough for ceiling joists but that still need extra stability. They are typically installed on every other rafter.

Eaves and Soffits

An eave is the area where rafters extend down from the ridge to meet the top plate. A soffit is created where rafters extend past the walls of a structure to create an open space below the eave. Rafter ends may be covered with fascia, and the soffit may be left open or enclosed, as shown below. The area where the roof meets the gable end wall is sometimes called the rake. Many buildings have overhangs on the gable ends. These overhangs are constructed of ladder-like frames or blocking called outriggers.

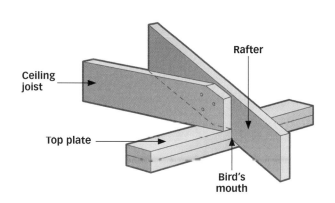

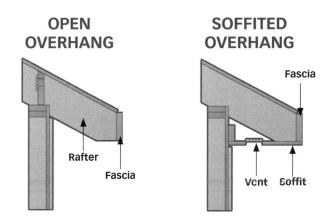

OPEN OVERHANG

SOFFITED OVERHANG

Trusses

Especially for larger structures, the alternative to building a stick-framed roof is to use prefabricated trusses. Well-designed trusses eliminate the need for load-bearing partitions below and greatly simplify framing so the roof can be put up quickly. One disadvantage to using roof trusses is the loss of attic space.

All trusses consist of three main parts: upper chords serving as rafters, lower chords acting as ceiling joists, and web members that tie the chords together. The parts are typically held together with metal or wood gusset plates. Different truss designs have different span potentials.

Engineered trusses can be ordered through most full-service lumberyards, but plan for possible long lead times. You will need to supply the dimensions, pitch, and style of roof—all information you should have on your plan.

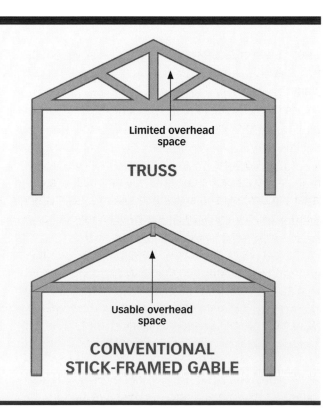

Framing a Roof

Three cuts are needed to make the classic rafter: a plumb cut where the rafter meets the ridge board, a plumb cut at the eave end, and a bird's mouth (a notch in the rafter—see page 77) that allows the rafter to fit on the top plate of the wall. Expect some trial and error. Depending on your plan, you may need to add ceiling joists or collar ties. If you do, cut them to length and install them when framing the roof.

1 MAKE A RAFTER TEMPLATE

The most precise and efficient way to cut rafters is to make a test rafter from a piece of rafter stock (for sheds, typically a 2 by 4 or 2 by 6). Consult your plans and carefully make the top and bottom plumb cuts and the bird's mouth. After you have made the test rafter, cut a second one. Working with a helper, hold the rafter in position temporarily with a scrap of 2-by material in between to serve as a ridge board and check the fit. If everything is correct, make your best rafter into a jig by tacking scraps of wood along one edge as shown. Then use it to mark the remaining rafters quickly and accurately.

2 MARK THE TOP PLATES

Measure and mark the position of the rafters on the double top plates, making sure to start at the same end where you began measuring the wall studs. This ensures that rafters with the same spacing will be directly over the studs. Trim the ridge board to length and transfer the rafter layout from the double top plates to the ridge board.

3 INSTALL THE RAFTERS

End-nail the first rafter to the ridge board, then toenail its mirror-image rafter to the opposite side of the ridge board. Lift the assembly into place so that the bird's mouth notches fit over the double top plates (applies to small roofs—large roofs are assembled in place and may require staging). A helper will need to support the opposite end of the ridge board while you check it for level and add a brace to hold it in place. Attach each rafter in its marked position on the double top plate with 16d nails. Add the rafters at the opposite end and continue until the roof framing is complete.

4 ADD FASCIA Fascia covers the ends of the rafters to protect them and provide a more finished look. A common fascia material is 5/4 or 1-by-6 primed pine. You may also add 2-by-4 subfascia boards nailed across the rafter ends (adjusted for length) before installing the trim fascia to add support for roof sheathing. Depending on your shed plans, you may want to cover the gable-end rafters with fascia as well. Secure the fascia to each rafter end with 8d galvanized finish nails.

Cutting a Bird's Mouth

One way to scribe a bird's mouth is to have a helper hold the top end of a rafter against a scrap of ridge board (at the right height) that's temporarily supported with vertical braces. Simultaneously, you will hold its tail against the end of the top plate and draw around it to mark the notch.

Your framing square can also be used to mark the bird's-mouth cut on a rafter. For example, let's say that your roof has a 4:12 slope.

Lay your square with the manufacturer's name up (the face) on the rafter. Locate 4 inches on the tongue (short arm), which represents the rise. Locate 12 inches on the blade (long arm), which represents the run. Holding the square in place, trace those lines to form the bird's-mouth notch. Using a circular saw with the blade set for maximum depth, make the bird's-mouth cuts, stopping just short of where the lines intersect. Do not overcut, or it can weaken the rafter. Complete the cuts with a handsaw. If necessary, use a sharp chisel to clean up any rough edges, allowing the notch to lie flat on the top plate.

Adding Asphalt Shingles

Asphalt shingles are inexpensive, easy to apply, and long lasting. (For details on roofing products, see pages 48–49.) Before you install them, you'll need to sheath the roof with plywood. Avoid anything less than ½ inch thick, or it won't provide a solid nailing base. For simple sheds with no interior finishes, you may want to use thicker sheathing (up to 1¼ inch) to avoid having the roofing nails show on the underside of the roof. The most critical part of installing shingles is the starter course. This course is placed with the tabs up instead of down to position the adhesive strip so it will help secure the first full row to the roof.

1 INSTALL SHEATHING
Install plywood sheathing over the roof framing, beginning at the bottom corner of one side. Place the face grain perpendicular to the rafters, trimming the sheets as necessary so that the ends are centered on rafters. Leave a ⅛-inch expansion gap between panels, and secure the panels to the rafters with 8d galvanized nails every 6 inches along the ends and every 12 inches elsewhere. Start the second row with a half sheet to offset the seams. Add panels until the entire roof is sheathed.

2 ROLL OUT ROOFING FELT
A layer of roofing felt (also called tar paper) over the sheathing protects the roofing from moisture. Lay out the first row of 36-inch-wide felt by snapping a chalk line 35⅝ inches above the eave (this provides a ⅜-inch overhang). Allow two inches of overlap for each row, snapping each successive line at 34 inches. Apply strips from the bottom up, aligning them with the chalk lines. Where two strips meet at a vertical seam, overlap them at least 4 inches. Use only enough staples or nails to hold the felt in place until the shingles can be installed.

3 ADD THE DRIP EDGE AND FLASHING
Before installing the asphalt shingles, protect the edges of the roof with drip edge. Drip edge is malleable aluminum that's preformed into a right angle with a lip along one edge to direct water away from the fascia and exterior siding. Attach the drip edge directly to the roof sheathing at the eave with the felt lapping over it. On the rake, the drip edge is applied over the felt. Check local codes. Secure the drip edge every 12 inches or so with roofing nails. Remember to install flashing in valleys, where your roof intersects with a vertical wall, on edges of rakes, and around all openings (see page 49).

Building Tip: To save time, leave overhang at the gable ends. Come back when the side of the roof is complete and do the trimming all at once using a sharp utility knife or a pair of heavy-duty shears.

4 INSTALL A STARTER COURSE

Once they're heated by the sun, asphalt shingles fuse together because of the pre-applied, self-healing mastic on the back. In order for the first full course of shingles to adhere to the front edge of the roof, a starter row is installed. The starter row consists of 7-inch strips cut from full shingles and installed upside down (with the tabs cut off) along the eaves. Because all additional rows of shingles use the starter row as a reference point, it needs to be straight. Start by snapping a chalk line on the felt to mark the top of the starter course. Secure the starter row with roofing nails 3 inches above the eaves. Precut starter strips may also be available.

5 ADD STANDARD COURSES

The remaining courses are all installed with the tabs pointing down. Install the first course of shingles on top of the starter row, with a ½-inch overhang to divert water away from the fascia. Check the manufacturer's recommended exposure, or amount of shingle not covered by the row above it. Use that measurement to snap a chalk line from the bottom of the first course to the installation line for the second course, offsetting it horizontally by half a tab. Continue snapping reference lines and adding courses until you reach the ridge. It's critical that the ends and the tab notches never line up with the shingle course below.

6 ATTACH THE RIDGE CAP

At the ridge, use readymade ridge shingles or cut your own 12-inch squares from standard shingles. Snap a line that's parallel to and 6 inches down from the ridge. Starting at the end opposite the prevailing wind, apply the shingles along the chalk line, leaving a 5-inch exposure and nail on each side, 5½ inches from the butt and 1 inch from the outside edge.

SIDING

No matter what siding you've chosen for the exterior of your new building, you'll need to check manufacturer's installation guidelines as well as building codes to determine whether you need to install sheathing as an underlayment. Sheathing is used under most siding materials to help brace the structure, as a solid base for nailing, and to improve insulation (see page 54).

PLYWOOD SIDING

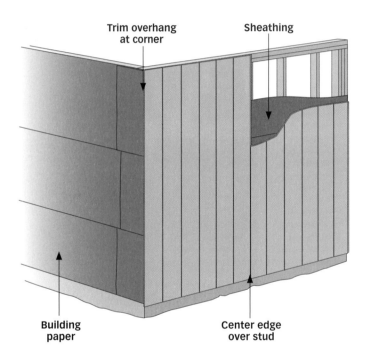

Trim overhang at corner

Sheathing

Building paper

Center edge over stud

Sheathing can be installed horizontally or vertically. Vertical sheathing works best for 8-foot walls because it can be nailed along all four edges. Position each sheet so the edges are centered on the studs. Nail sheets to the studs with 8d nails every 6 inches along the edge and every 12 inches elsewhere. Leave a $\frac{1}{8}$-inch expansion gap between panels. Many local codes require a layer of either building paper or house wrap over the sheathing. This moisture barrier gives your structure an extra layer of protection.

Plywood siding goes up quickly and often does double duty as sheathing. For instructions on how to install traditional solid-board siding, see pages 82–83. Other commonly used options are fiber-cement, plywood lap boards, and

Clean Cuts in Sheet Products

To make clean, straight cuts in plywood and other sheet materials, clamp a straightedge to the sheet as a guide for your saw.

If you're using a circular saw, measure the distance from the edge of the saw's base plate to the blade, and clamp the straightedge at this distance from the cutting line.

Be sure to support the sheet on sawhorses, adding two long boards under each side of the cut line. When you're using a circular saw or jigsaw, cut the sheets on the back side to avoid splintering the face.

metal. Windows and doors with external flanges or brick molding are normally installed after sheathing is on but before siding is attached. Units without flanges can be added after the siding is on (see pages 84–85).

Installing Sheet Siding

Plywood siding installed without sheathing must be at least ⅜ inch thick over studs 16 inches on center, and at least ½ inch thick over studs on 24-inch centers. Panels as thin as ⁵⁄₁₆ inch may be applied over sheathing. Plywood can be mounted vertically or horizontally. If you choose a horizontal pattern, stagger vertical end joints and nail the long, horizontal edges into fire blocks (2-by-4 blocks nailed between the studs) or other nailing supports to make sure the joints are protected. Any joint that is not sealed or shiplapped or does not have a batten should be primed and caulked with mastic.

VERTICAL JOINTS

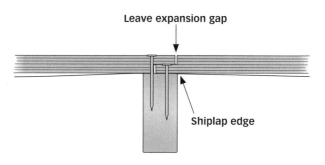

Plywood · Butt and caulk · Back with building paper · Wall stud

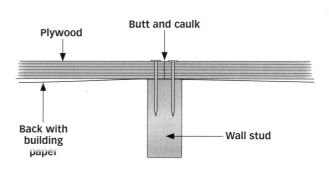

Leave expansion gap · Shiplap edge

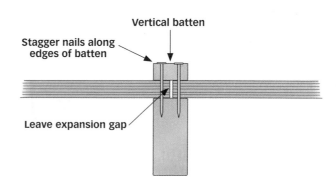

Vertical batten · Stagger nails along edges of batten · Leave expansion gap

1 INSTALL THE FIRST SHEET A general layout of all the sheets is necessary to avoid strips that are too narrow, especially near doors and windows. The first sheet almost always requires a vertical cut. Align the first sheet vertically so its edge is ¼ inch shy of the corner (it will be covered by the corner trimboards). Check that the opposite edge reaches the center of a wall stud, and make sure the edge is plumb; shift the panel and trim as necessary. Attach the siding to the studs using 8d galvanized nails every 6 inches along the perimeter and every 12 inches elsewhere.

2 ADD REMAINING SHEETS Install remaining sheets, leaving a ⅛-inch expansion gap between them. Some panels have shiplap edges; nail them as shown at right. If your plywood doesn't have these edges, simply butt and caulk the joints or cover them with vertical battens. Vertical installations with one sheet installed above the other require Z flashing between sheets.

Applying Solid-board Siding

Many board sidings seem similar, but treat each pattern individually and obtain installation specifications from the supplier. Check local code, as some board siding requires sheathing, while other types may not. With beveled or clapboard siding, windows and doors are installed first, with trim and casings added after so the siding butts snugly into the trim without gaps. Flat siding can be installed first and trim added later. Some patterns may be installed vertically, horizontally, or even diagonally, while others are limited to one direction.

Decide on the corner treatment you want to use before nailing up any siding (see page 83). Corner boards should lie flat against the siding. Mitered corners need to be cut and fitted precisely to avoid gaps where water can collect. Plan the layout of your siding so that horizontal courses run continuously above and below windows and doors without notching. Nailing patterns are very important and should comply with the siding manufacturer's recommendations. Butt joints in siding runs should fall over a stud.

SOLID-BOARD SIDING

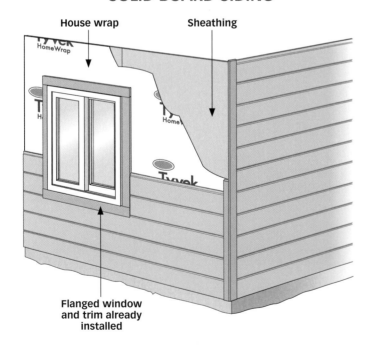

House wrap

Sheathing

Flanged window and trim already installed

1 ATTACH MOISTURE BARRIER To prevent heat loss and damage from moisture, wrap your sheathed structure in house wrap or building paper. Minimize seams, providing at least a 12-inch overlap when necessary. Leave excess around window and door openings and wrap it around the opening to create a seal. For details, see page 86.

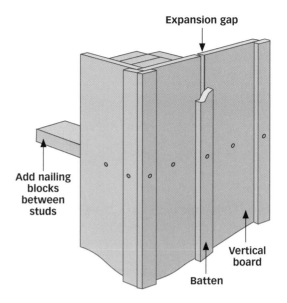

Expansion gap

Add nailing blocks between studs

Vertical board

Batten

2 START NAILING ON SIDING

When working with horizontal clapboard siding, nail on any inside and outside corner pieces first, as well as window and door casings (see page 87). Snap a level line to mark the top of the base course and nail a small starter strip along the bottom edge of the sheathing to give the siding the proper pitch. Align the base course with the chalk line and nail it in place. Overlap the next piece and repeat as you move up the wall. Check the siding periodically for level and adjust the following courses gradually to bring things back in line. Beveled siding that is 6 inches wide should have at least one inch of overlap. Siding 8 inches or wider should have 1 to 1½ inches or the amount specified by the manufacturer.

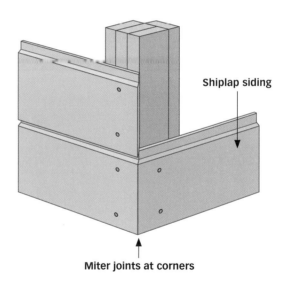

Shiplap siding

Miter joints at corners

Building Tip: For some siding installations, pre-drilling holes will prevent splintering of the wood.

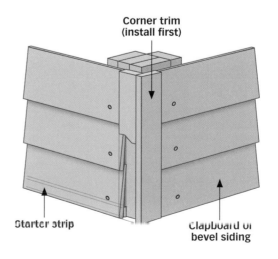

Corner trim (install first)

Starter strip

Clapboard or bevel siding

WINDOWS AND DOORS

Assuming you've done a great job of sizing the rough openings (see page 70), installing a manufactured window or door is pretty straightforward. Essentially, the job consists of centering the door or window frame in the opening, shimming it level and plumb, and securing it to the framing.

Flanged windows and doors are normally installed after any sheathing is on but before siding is attached. Windows and doors with attached casings, or brick mold, are typically installed before bevel siding (or any siding that does not have a flat profile) but after flat siding like plywood. Units without flanges or casings can be added once the siding is on. Your supplier is a great resource and can suggest the best installation method for your chosen products.

DOOR ANATOMY

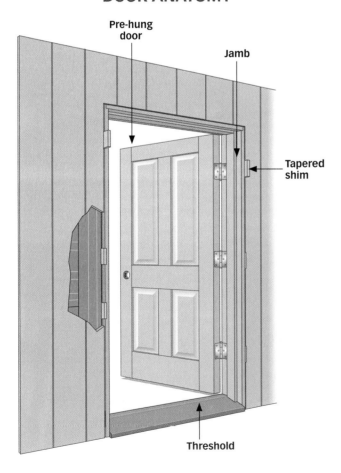

Pre-hung door

Jamb

Tapered shim

Threshold

Build Your Own Door

Several projects in Chapter 4 call for doors you make yourself. Although you could choose traditional door makers' joints like mortise-and-tenon, the simplest way to build shed doors is in layers. The outer face of the door is often made of the same siding material as the building, with an added support frame on the back side.

The Z-frame shown here is a good choice for joining vertical boards. First, lay out the boards face up and pick the order you like. Then flip the boards facedown, snug them together, and lay out the bracing as shown at left. Secure the braces with nails or screws (we used stainless-steel screws) that are slightly shorter than the combined thickness of the parts. If you like, first add a bead of exterior glue to the backs of the braces. You may also want to add trim or molding to the front of the door as a last step.

Installing a Pre-hung Door

Installing a door the old-fashioned way means constructing a door frame, attaching it to the rough opening, hinging the door to the frame, and installing a latch or lockset. If you buy a pre-hung door, much of the work has been done for you. The jambs are assembled, the door is hinged to the jamb, and on exterior pre-hung doors, the threshold is typically in place. The only tricky part is making sure that the unit is level and plumb and that the frame doesn't bow or twist as you install it. Check and recheck before securing the unit to the framing. When ordering a pre-hung door, be prepared to specify many options, including door swing, hardware finish, depth of framing, type of predrilled holes you want for the lock you're using, and type of threshold.

Shim Strategy

Fine-tune the fit of a door or window within an oversize rough opening using pairs of tapered wood shims. Tap in a pair of shims, one on each side, until they are snug against the jambs. Then nail through the jambs and both shims into the framing. Score thin shims with a utility knife and snap them off flush with the jambs. Trim thicker ones with a reciprocating saw or a handsaw.

1 POSITION THE DOOR

Slide the pre-hung unit into the rough opening and center it all around. If you plan to add an interior finish floor later, raise the doorjambs above the subfloor with scrap blocks the same thickness as the finish flooring.

2 SHIM IT PLUMB AND LEVEL

Insert pairs of tapered shims along the perimeter, tapping them in place between the jambs and the trimmer studs or header. Adjust the shims as necessary to make the unit plumb and level.

3 NAIL THE DOOR TO THE FRAMING

To secure the frame, drive galvanized finish nails through the interior jambs and shims and into the trimmer studs and header. Secure doors with nailing flanges or pre-installed brick mold from the outside.

Installing a Window

In general, attach wood windows to the sheathing by nailing through the exterior casing, or brick mold, on the outside. For aluminum, clad, or vinyl windows, drive nails or screws through the factory-installed nailing flanges on the outside perimeter of the window. If your window has neither casing nor flanges, secure it through the interior jambs and into the trimmer studs, header, and rough sill surrounding the opening. Exact installation methods vary, so always follow the manufacturer's recommendations.

1 CUT OUT THE OPENING
If you've already applied plywood sheathing or siding, you'll need to remove it from the rough opening. From inside the structure, drill ¾-inch access holes through the sheathing at the corners of the rough opening. Use a reciprocating saw (as shown) or jigsaw to cut the opening.

2 APPLY MOISTURE BARRIER
If you're using house wrap or building felt, wrap edges into window and door openings, as shown. The best practice is to make diagonal cuts in the house wrap at the top corners so the window flange can be tucked beneath the house wrap. Once the window is installed, seal the perimeter with a peel-and-stick membrane, such as Vycor, as shown in the drawing on the facing page.

3 INSTALL THE WINDOW
Before you place the window in the opening, run a bead of exterior-grade caulk along the perimeter. From inside, raise the window to the correct height above the rough sill with shims. Check the top of the unit with a carpenter's level. Next, slip pairs of tapered shims between the jamb and the framed opening, following the manufacturer's instructions. Check for level and plumb. For windows with attached exterior trim or brick mold, drive galvanized finish nails through the trim and into the framing. With nailing flanges, use either headed nails or screws. For windows without trim or flanges, drive finish nails through the jambs at the shim locations and into the framing.

Finishing Off with Trim

To complete your shed's exterior, install trim around windows and doors and along the top and/or bottom of the exterior walls if desired. Trim can be minimal or elaborate, and joints can be either butted (as shown here) or mitered. For exterior trim, 1-by-4 redwood or cedar works well but can be pricey. Pine is a less expensive option. Use pre-primed trim to make painting quick and easy. Otherwise, it's best to prime the backs of the boards before applying them. A power miter saw (see page 43) makes quick, clean, and accurate cuts.

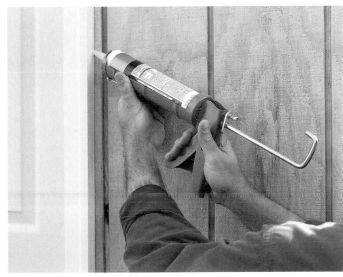

1 APPLY TRIM Be sure to use galvanized finish nails that are long enough to penetrate the siding, the sheathing, and the rough framing below. Leave the nail heads about 1/8 inch above the wood and finish driving them in with a nail set.

2 SEAL THE JOINTS Complete your window or door trim by running a bead of silicone caulk around the exterior trim to create a watertight seal.

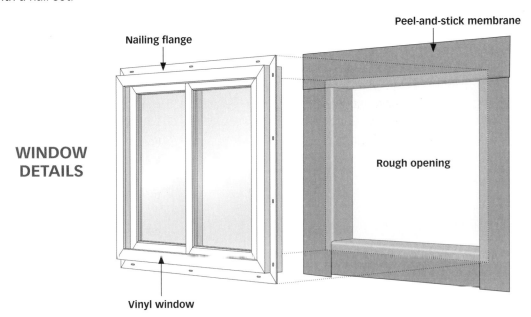

WINDOW DETAILS

Nailing flange

Peel-and-stick membrane

Rough opening

Vinyl window

SYSTEMS

Your project is really taking shape. You have a roof on your structure, and the exterior walls are up. If you plan to incorporate electrical and plumbing systems, now is the time to make sure they are in place.

Adding Power

Any shed, garage, or barn will be more functional and flexible if you run power to it. You will be able to light up the interior at night, use power tools and appliances—even install heating and cooling. Getting the power there is the tough part; adding interior wiring is simpler.

Though you could run overhead wires to your shed, it's far better to run power underground (marked red below) from your home's service panel. First have a licensed electrician check to make sure you have sufficient capacity at the service panel. If not, you may need to upgrade the panel—a potentially pricey proposition. With the power source established, you can dig a trench (check local codes for the required depth), bury UF (underground feeder) cable, or run separate wires in metal or plastic conduit.

Depending on your power needs, you may run a single 20-amp circuit that ends in a junction box, a 40-to-60-amp

cable feeding a subpanel, or up to a 100-amp line that powers a new service panel. From this source, the wiring branches out into circuits—a single branch for an overhead light and a couple of receptacles, or multiple branches. Nonmetallic (NM) cable makes interior wiring simple, since no conduit is required. You simply route the cable through ceilings and walls through holes in studs or joists. Be sure to check local codes for guidelines and consider the function of your building before making a plan. If your interior is unfinished, you may still want to run electrical lines in conduit for safety, function, and a neater appearance.

Electrical codes specify everything from how high a receptacle is mounted to the number of wires in a junction box. Making final connections to a subpanel or service panel is best done by a licensed electrician. Make sure to have the wiring inspected before adding any wall coverings.

OUTBUILDING ELECTRICAL SYSTEM

Garage door opener

120-volt receptacle

Floodlight

Middle-of-run receptacle

End-of-run receptacle

Subpanel

40–60-amp line from house

Running Plumbing

As convenient as it is to have running water in a shed, garage, or barn, it may not be feasible. A small budget might rule it out, and your local climate may also limit your options.

In warm climates, you might get by with burying a garden hose a few inches below the lawn, then making a simple drain pit to serve as the septic or sewer. In colder climates, water and waste lines must be installed well below the frost line—in some areas as much as 4 to 5 feet deep. Pipe depth, materials, and even who can make the connections will be defined by local code.

In a typical outbuilding, a single cold-water line is run from the house. Likewise, a waste line runs out to the building, but it slopes back toward the house so it will drain into the existing system.

At the new structure, the waste line terminates in a sanitary tee with a cleanout port.

A vent pipe connects to the top of the sanitary tee and continues up through the roof. Another drainpipe connects to the sink via a trap. Here again, the piping must slope down toward the tee to allow drainage. A shutoff valve on the water supply line controls water flow to the sink faucet. If you want hot water, don't try to run an insulated line. Install a water heater in the outbuilding instead. See Sunset's *You Can Build: Plumbing* for more information.

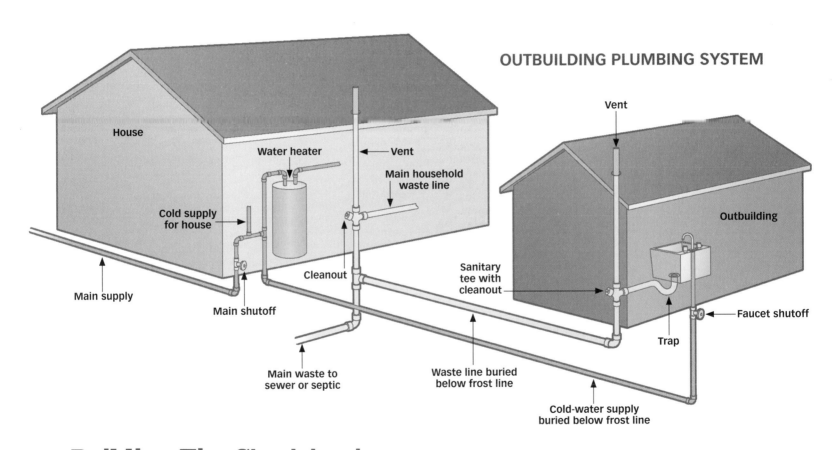

OUTBUILDING PLUMBING SYSTEM

House

Water heater

Vent

Cold supply for house

Main household waste line

Main supply

Main shutoff

Cleanout

Main waste to sewer or septic

Sanitary tee with cleanout

Waste line buried below frost line

Cold-water supply buried below frost line

Vent

Outbuilding

Trap

Faucet shutoff

Building Tip: Check local requirements for getting power or water to your building before breaking ground.

FINISHING TOUCHES

After any electrical and plumbing systems are in place and have passed inspection, you are ready to tackle the finish work. This might include adding insulation, drywall, and trim. Your building might also need a set of stairs or an access ramp.

Adding Insulation

Interior walls can be left bare or covered. Finishing off a ceiling or an interior wall usually begins with the installation of insulation. Then the wall or ceiling coverings are attached to the framing. Wall coverings around windows and doors should butt closely against the window or door jamb. Fill any gaps with insulating foam or scraps of fiberglass to prevent drafts. To add trim around these openings, see pages 92–93.

INTERIOR WALL DETAILS

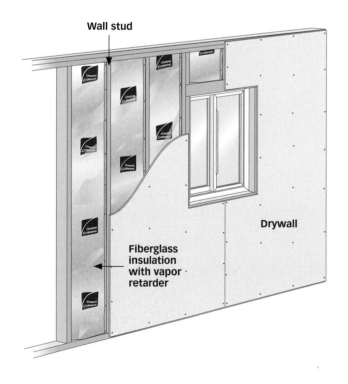

Wall stud

Drywall

Fiberglass insulation with vapor retarder

INSTALLING FIBERGLASS

Measure from top to bottom, add 3 inches, and cut a strip of insulation to length with scissors or a utility knife. Be sure to wear gloves, a dust mask, and protective clothing. Press the strip between the framing and overlap the facing onto the framing. Begin stapling at the top and work your way down both sides.

INSTALLING RIGID FOAM

Precut strips of rigid foam make installation a snap. Measure between top and bottom and cut the strip to match with a utility knife or a handsaw. For walls, it's best to apply a bead of construction adhesive along the perimeter of the foam to hold it until the wall covering is installed. On ceilings, first apply a generous bead of construction adhesive along the perimeter and an X from top to bottom, then press the strip into place.

Installing Drywall

Drywall, or gypsum wallboard, is often used for covering both walls and ceilings. Position the first sheet of drywall tight in a corner so the opposite edge is centered on a framing member. Wall sheets may be installed either vertically or horizontally. If the opposite edge of the sheet isn't centered on the studs, remove and trim it, as shown below.

1 SECURE SHEET TO FRAMING

Drywall nails go in quickly, but they have a tendency to "pop" over time as the studs dry out. Drywall screws are stronger. Drive them so they sit just below the surface without breaking the paper covering.

2 APPLY TAPE

To conceal the joints between sheets, apply drywall tape over the seams. Tape may be adhesive or nonstick. To apply nonstick tape, spread on a thin amount of joint compound over the seam, then gently press the tape into the compound with a wide-blade putty knife.

3 ADD JOINT COMPOUND

Apply a first full coat of joint compound over both the tape and the dimples left by the screws, using a 4-to-6-inch-wide drywall knife. Spread the compound as smoothly as possible so that sanding will remove only minor imperfections.

4 FEATHER AND SMOOTH

Once the compound is dry, apply a second coat with a wider drywall knife, gently feathering the compound away from the joint for a smooth transition. Lightly sand while it's still wet, then do a final sanding when it's dry and use a slightly damp drywall sponge to level the surface.

Cutting Drywall

To trim drywall to size, draw a line with a straight-edge (a drywall T square is ideal) and cut along the line with a sharp utility knife. Flip the sheet over and bend back one end to snap the sheet. Run your utility knife along the inside crease to complete the cut. If necessary, smooth the cut edge with a rasp or file. A perforated rasp works best.

Installing Interior Window and Door Trim

Install interior window and door trim after wall coverings are in place. Typically, trim consists of two side casings and a head casing. Window trim may also include an apron and a finish sill. All these components are shown in the drawing at right. Some windows—especially flanged vinyl models—won't fill the entire depth of the opening, leaving some rough framing exposed. To trim out this gap, you'll need to add manufactured extension jambs or other strips of wood, as shown below.

WINDOW TRIM

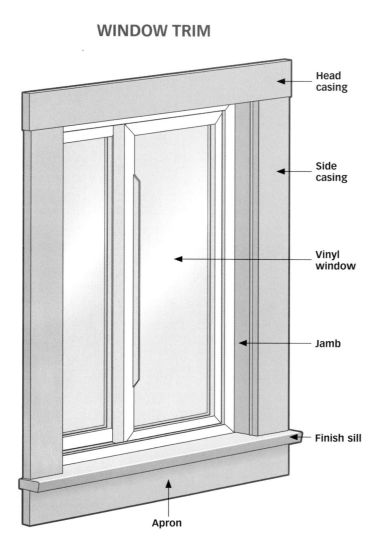

Head casing

Side casing

Vinyl window

Jamb

Finish sill

Apron

Adding a Finish Sill

If you like the look of an interior finish sill (also called a stool) below your window, install it before adding the other trim. The trick is to notch the sill around the window jamb and wall covering as shown. Cut the notches with a jigsaw (see page 43) or a handsaw. Normally the sill extends slightly past the outside edges of the side casings. Nail the finish sill to the rough sill below.

With the sill in place, cut and attach side and head casings. Note that even if your top casing joints are mitered, the bottoms of the side casings will be square where they meet the sill. Finally, cut and attach the apron, as shown below. Typically, the apron lines up with the outside edges of the side casings, allowing the sill to extend beyond it. Nail the apron to the wall framing, then drill pilot holes and drive a few more finish nails through the sill into the edge of the apron.

1 INSULATE AROUND THE OPENING
If you are insulating your structure, take the time to add extra fiberglass insulation in any gaps between the window or door jamb and the framing. This should be done before you add the interior trim to help reduce drafts and heat loss.

2 MARK THE REVEAL
Draw a setback line, or reveal, about ¼ inch in from the inside edges of the window or door jamb. Align each of the side casings with this line and mark them where they intersect the top reveal line.

3 ADD THE SIDE TRIM
Cut the head and side casings to length with a power miter saw or a handsaw and a miter box. You can use either 45-degree miter joints, as shown in step 4, or butt joints (see drawing on page 92). Tack the side casings in place with 2-inch finish nails, aligning the inside edges with the reveal lines.

4 INSTALL THE TOP TRIM
Now nail the head casing into place. When attaching trim with nails, stop hammering when the head of the nail is about ⅛ inch from the surface. Finish driving the nail using a nail set. Set the nails about 1/16 inch below the surface, fill with putty, and sand flush when dry. Fill any gaps between the trim and the wall with paintable latex caulk.

Adding Stairs or Ramps

Stairs or ramps must attach securely to your shed, garage, or barn with a ledger board and joist hangers. The lower stair or the bottom of the ramp should rest on a concrete or compacted gravel footing. Check your local building code to verify what kind of footings you'll need and whether or not a handrail is required.

STAIRS

Typical shed stairs consist of two or three stringers and treads. To make your own, first establish the rise and run of the steps. Total rise is the distance from the ground to the floor of the structure; unit rise is the height of each step. Total run (how far the steps will extend out) requires a little math.

Start by dividing the total rise by 7 inches (the recommended rise or height of each step) to find out how many steps you'll need and round up. Then, to find total run, multiply the unit run (or tread depth) you'd like by the number of treads—which is always one less than the number of steps. It's safest when treads are at least 10 inches deep. For example, a total rise of 40 inches divided by 7 inches equals 5.7, so rounding up yields 6 steps (5 treads). The total run in this case would be at least 5 times 10 inches, or 50 inches. To find your actual unit rise, divide your measured total rise by the number of steps. In this example, actual unit rise equals 40 inches divided by 6—roughly $6\frac{5}{8}$ inches.

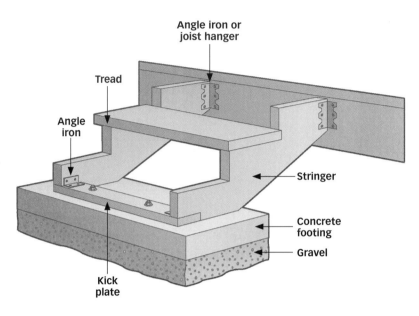

Angle iron or joist hanger

Tread

Angle iron

Stringer

Concrete footing

Gravel

Kick plate

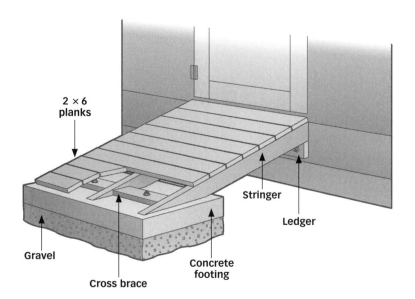

2 × 6 planks

Stringer

Ledger

Gravel

Cross brace

Concrete footing

RAMP

A ramp is easier to build than stairs because no treads are involved. All you need to do is decide on the slope of the ramp and cut the ends of the stringers accordingly. The slope is measured in inches of vertical rise per linear foot. A 1-in-8 slope will do for most utility work. For wheelchair access, use a 1-in-12 slope.

Building Platform Steps

If your rise is modest and it's more convenient to have stairs that can be accessed from the front and sides, consider a set of platform steps—basically a stack of interconnecting boxes built atop a firm footing. Each box is a simple wood frame (2 by 6s work well) topped with additional lumber. Each box should be no more than 7 inches tall. The width and depth of the stairs can vary, but they should be based on some multiple of a typical stride.

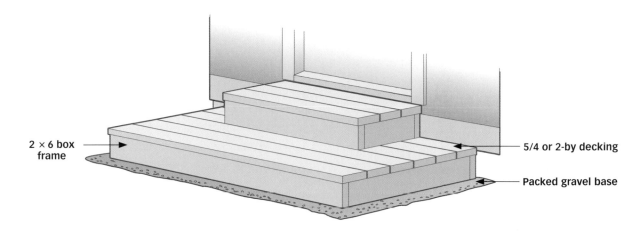

2 × 6 box frame

5/4 or 2-by decking

Packed gravel base

1 BUILD THE FRAMES First, cut front and back frame pieces to length for each step, then ends and internal dividers (space these no more than 16 inches apart). Screw or nail the pieces together.

2 ADD TREADS Top each platform with 5/4 or 2-by treads. This example shows 5/4-by-6 composite decking, and the steps were sized so that the treads are flush in back but overlap the frame about an inch in front and on each side. Use screws to secure treads to the front, back, and internal dividers of each frame. Countersink, or recess, the screws below the surface. If using composite decking, follow the installation guidelines carefully and use only the recommended board spacing and fasteners.

3 SECURE THE PLATFORMS Secure each frame to the one below it with screws driven through the frames at an angle, as shown. Or, if you'd rather hide these fasteners, make connections on the insides of the frames before adding the top treads. Finally, secure the platform to the shed's wall or floor framing with the fasteners specified in your local building code.

PROJECTS

Here are drawings and step-by-step instructions to create a structure suitable for a wide range of backyard spaces, from a tiny utility shed to a sizable storage barn.

UTILITY SHED

Designed to stand against the wall of a house or garage, or against a fence, this cedar utility shed provides covered storage without taking up valuable yard space. Simple to build and customize, it easily holds sports equipment like golf clubs and bicycles, or gardening supplies.

MATERIALS LIST

2 × 4 rafters, blocking, and wall framing

Pressure-treated 2 × 4s for floor frame

1 × 3 cedar trim

¾" exterior plywood for floor

1 × 4 cedar fascia

1 × 6 beveled cedar siding

½" taper-sawn cedar shakes for roof

15-lb. roof felt

½" exterior-grade plywood roof sheathing

1 × 6 cedar for door

1 × 2 cedar for door stop

Ceramic coated screws

Galvanized nails

Black powder-coated steel hinges, handle, and hasp

⅛" plexiglass for window

2 × 2 and 1 × 1 cedar for window frame

Design Details

This lean-to shed measures 3 by 6 feet but is easy to expand in width or length with standard 2-by-4 framing. The door can be moved to either end wall. Substituting an operable window for the fixed one shown here or adding windows increases light and ventilation. If you are building your shed against another structure and applying a final finish to the exterior, be sure to frame, sheath, and finish the rear wall first while it is easy to access, then attach it to the floor frame.

Design by Cedarshed. To order plans for this project, see page 190.

Building Tip: If your lean-to shed needs to fit tightly against another structure, eliminate the roof overhang in the back.

continued »

How to Build the Utility Shed

The floor frame for this small shed is set on paving blocks. Excavate an area slightly larger than the shed's footprint to a depth of 4 inches, replace with compacted, crushed rock, and level (see page 64). Set four paving blocks in the corners of a rectangle measuring 5 feet 11 inches by 2 feet 10 inches. Add another block centered on each of the long sides. Construct the floor frame and level in place. Be sure to build, sheath, and finish the walls as needed before assembling.

1 FRAME THE FLOOR With the level concrete pavers in place, frame the floor using pressure-treated 2 by 4s 16 inches on center. Sheath the floor frame in ¾-inch exterior plywood, move it into place, and level carefully.

UTILITY FOUNDATION & FLOOR DETAIL

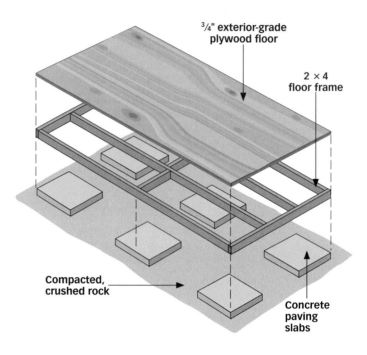

¾" exterior-grade plywood floor

2 × 4 floor frame

Compacted, crushed rock

Concrete paving slabs

UTILTIY WALL DETAIL

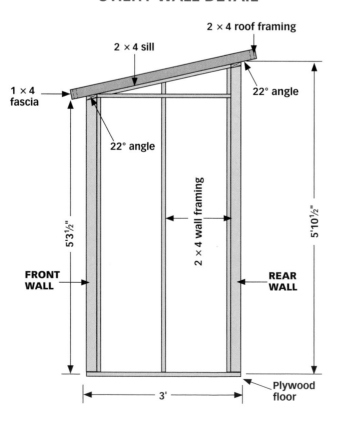

2 × 4 roof framing

2 × 4 sill

1 × 4 fascia

22° angle

22° angle

2 × 4 wall framing

5'3½"

5'10½"

FRONT WALL

REAR WALL

Plywood floor

3'

2 BUILD THE WALLS Build the rear wall of the shed first. The wall measures 71 inches wide by 70½ inches high overall. Cut a 22-degree angle at the top end of each stud before installing the top plate. Add the 1-by-3 exterior trim to each corner stud and install the beveled siding. Apply finish if needed and install the wall on the floor frame, bracing as necessary (see page 72). Frame the front wall 63½ inches high with the same 22-degree angle and rough openings for the window (16¼ inches wide by 25¼ inches high) and door (31½ inches by 57¼ inches). Use doubled 2 by 4s as headers (see page 71). Add cripple studs (see page 70), raise the wall, and brace it. Build the side walls 63½ inches high and set in place, leaving a gap between the top sill and the rafter location. When all the wall sections are plumb and square, screw the corners together and remove the bracing.

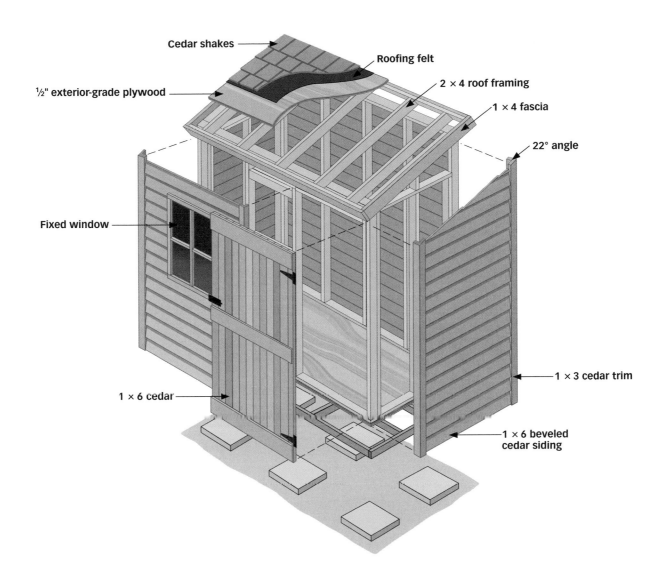

Cedar shakes

Roofing felt

½" exterior-grade plywood

2 × 4 roof framing

1 × 4 fascia

22° angle

Fixed window

1 × 3 cedar trim

1 × 6 cedar

1 × 6 beveled
cedar siding

3 FRAME AND INSTALL THE ROOF

Cut 2-by-4 roof rafters 41½ inches long and 24 inches on center. Toenail them to both top plates (see page 72), overhanging the front and back of the shed by 3¾ inches. Add a gable stud on each end to fit between the end rafter and the top plate. Block the openings between each rafter with 2 by 4s (see page 109). Install the 1-by-4 fascia and sheath the roof with ½-inch exterior plywood and a layer of roofing felt. Install the cedar shake roof. For more on roofing techniques, see pages 74–79.

4 ADD TRIM AND ENCLOSE THE WALLS

Add the corner, window, and door trim. Plan for the installation of the hasp (lockable clasp for the door) by installing a mounting block prior to siding. Install the beveled cedar siding on the remaining three sides of the shed (see pages 82–83).

5 BUILD AND INSTALL THE WINDOW AND DOOR

Build a 2-by-2 cedar frame to fit the rough window opening. Attach pre-cut plexiglass that's ¼ inch smaller than the frame to the back side, pre-drilling the holes. Using glue and screws, attach 1-by-1 cedar to the front of the plexiglass to create the window frame.

Install the window in the opening by screwing through the 2 by 2s into the frame. Build the 31-inch-wide-by-57¼-inch-high door out of 1-by-6 cedar (see page 84). Brace the back of the door with a Z-frame and then add trim pieces to the front as shown. Mount the door using the T-hinges and add the lock and handle. Add a 1-by-2-inch door stop to the inside edge of the door frame. Finish the exterior of the shed and add interior storage.

Measuring just 2 by 4 feet, this handy gardener's hutch fits discreetly under the eaves of a house or garage or in a corner of the garden. Dividing the interior into two sections makes it easy to store all of your garden tools. Inventory your small items and install shelves at just the right height on one side and stow taller shovels and rakes on the other. Build this hutch on a foundation of concrete pavers or treated timbers and frame the floor with pressure-treated 2 by 4s. Add a floor of 1-by-4 cedar and a roof of 1-by-6 grooved cedar paneling over roofing felt and framing. Double doors built of 1-by-6 cedar open wide for full access and are mounted on hinges attached to the door trim. Pre-assemble wall sections and doors, apply exterior finishes, and then install them in place. Customize this hutch by using an alternative siding or roofing material.

Design by Cedarshed. To order plans for this project, see page 190.

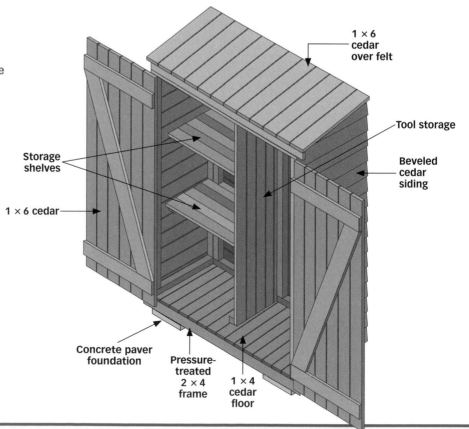

1 × 6 cedar over felt

Tool storage

Beveled cedar siding

Storage shelves

1 × 6 cedar

Concrete paver foundation

Pressure-treated 2 × 4 frame

1 × 4 cedar floor

RECYCLING CENTER

It can be challenging to find a space for your recycling bins that's convenient and attractive. Measuring just 40 by 48 inches, this cedar mini-shed can solve that problem and hold your recycling bin, garbage can, and a shelf of supplies as well.

Build the wood-framed floor on a foundation of concrete paving slabs and frame the walls and storage shelf using western red cedar. Then build the doors and sheath the roof with tongue-and-groove cedar. You can easily expand this shed to hold more bins or use it as a small tool storage shed.

Design by Cedarshed.
To order plans for this
project, see page 190.

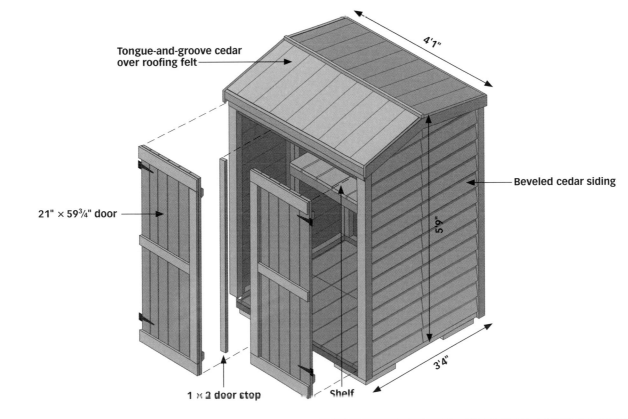

Tongue-and-groove cedar over roofing felt

4'7"

Beveled cedar siding

21" × 59¾" door

5'9"

1 × 2 door stop

Shelf

3'4"

SALTBOX SHED

The saltbox shed is a rural classic. Its rugged construction and ample headroom make it perfect for storing equipment or using as a potting shed. This 8-by-12-foot version features double doors and an entry ramp. Clean, simple lines, board-and-batten siding, and a metal roof give this shed its traditional design appeal.

MATERIALS LIST

- 4 × 6 pressure-treated skids
- 2 × 6 hemlock rim joists, floor joists, rafters
- ¾" CDX plywood
- 4 × 4 hemlock posts, beams, angle braces
- 2 × 4 hemlock wall framing
- 1 × 8 pine siding
- 1 × 12 pine siding, doors, bird blocking
- 2 × 6 pressure-treated stringers for ramp
- 5/4 × 6 pressure-treated decking for ramp
- 1 × 6 hemlock collar ties
- 1 × 4 hemlock roof strapping
- 1 × 8 hemlock ridge
- Metal roofing and ridge cap
- 1 × 4 pine trim
- 2 × 4 pine trim
- 2 × 8 pine fascia
- 1 × 8 pine fascia
- 1 × 2 pine door stop
- 1 × 3 pine window stops
- 12 × 12-inch wood louvered vent
- 2 × 2 light barn sash windows
- Hinges, turn latches, chain bolts, window hooks, eye hooks
- Galvanized nails, pan head screws, drywall screws, roofing screws

Design Details

This heavy-duty shed uses timber framing techniques (often called post-and-beam construction). However, instead of mortise-and-tenon joinery, simple half lap joints are used for attaching the 4-by-4 top plates to the corner posts. Ideally, this shed is built with rough-cut lumber that has not been planed, meaning that a 4-by-4 post actually measures a full 4 inches. If rough-cut lumber is not available in your area, you can use dimensional lumber and adjust the plans accordingly (see page 45). Since post-and-beam construction is easily adapted, you can add windows or change the door size as needed. As you look over the materials list, be aware that you may have to substitute regionally available lumber—for example, cedar trim and siding instead of pine. Your local lumber supplier can assist you in making choices.

Design by Jamaica Cottage Shop. To order plans for this project, see page 190.

Building Tip: To prevent warping, protect your building materials from the weather, especially trim, doors, and windows.

continued »

How to Build the Saltbox Shed

DECK PLAN DETAIL

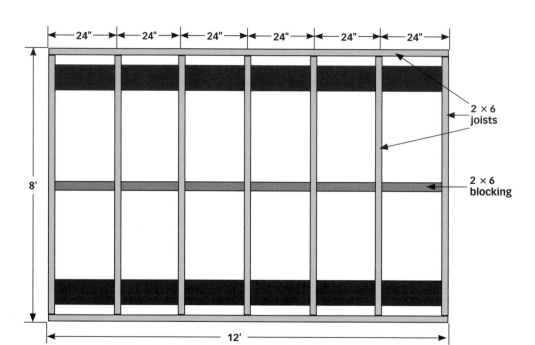

24"   24"   24"   24"   24"   24"

2 × 6 joists

2 × 6 blocking

8'

12'

Building Tip: When temporarily bracing walls, don't sink the nails, as they will be easier to remove later.

1 PREPARE THE SITE AND FOUNDATION

Level and install 3 to 4 inches of crushed rock a foot larger than the building on all sides. Position six 4-by-8-by-16-inch concrete blocks to form a 7-by-11-foot rectangle. Cut two 4-by-6 treated skids 12 feet long and bevel the ends. Set the skids roughly in position on the blocks with angled cuts facing down (see pages 62–65).

2 BUILD THE FLOOR

Position the 4-by-6 skids 6½ inches in from the framing. Cut 2-by-6 floor joists 7 feet 9 inches long. Add 2-by-6 rim joists and center blocking to form an 8-by-12-foot floor frame. Square the floor by measuring the diagonals and then toenail each joist to the skids below. Install the ¾-inch CDX plywood flooring and nail on the joist seams (see page 68).

3 SET THE CORNER POSTS

Set four corner posts on the floor platform. Prior to installation, cut the front posts 79 inches long and then cut a half lap joint in each post with the top of the joint at 71 inches and the bottom of the joint equaling the width of the post. To do this, use a handsaw or skill saw to make two cuts halfway through the post. Then turn and cut in from either side at the center of the post to extract the block, leaving you with a half lap joint (see illustration on page 107). Cut the two rear posts 67 inches long. Toenail the four posts onto the platform tight to the corners. The half lap joints should face the outside to accept the top plate. The nails should be set so that the siding will cover them, blind nailed, whenever possible (see illustration on page 108).

REAR WALL FRAME DETAIL

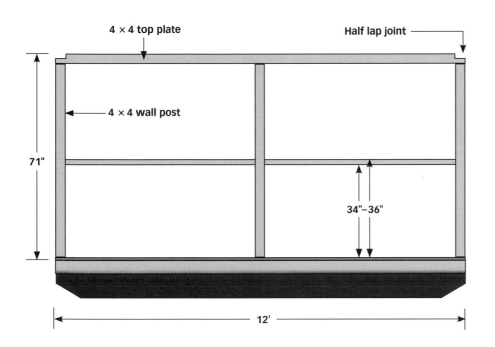

4 × 4 top plate

Half lap joint

4 × 4 wall post

71"

34"–36"

12'

HALF LAP JOINT DETAIL

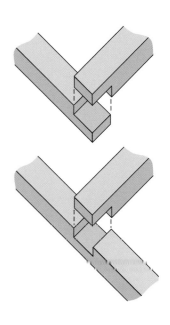

4 **BUILD THE WALLS** With post-and-beam construction, there is no bottom plate. Build the rear wall by attaching the 4-by-4 top plate after cutting half lap joints in the ends that face up. Nail through the half lap joints into the post below. Install the 4-by-4 center post and toenail it to the deck and top plate. Install the 2-by-4 horizontal nailer 34 inches high on either side of the center post. The height of the rear wall is 71 inches; the height of the front wall is 83 inches. Frame the two gable end walls accordingly using both measurements and install the top plate in the half lap joints on the front posts. Complete each gable end wall by adding the 2-by-4 nailer. Frame the front wall by installing the 4-by-4 top plate.

5 **INSTALL TEMPORARY BRACING** Recheck the level of the deck. Attach a brace spanning the front and rear walls exactly 12 feet long. Plumb the walls. Square and attach temporary bracing to all walls on the inside so it does not interfere with installation of the siding or rafters. This temporary bracing will remain in place until the shed is complete.

6 **FRAME THE FRONT BEARING WALL AND ADD ANGLE BRACING** Frame the rough opening of the door with 4-by-4 posts. Attach the 2-by-4 door header at 73 inches. Use 2 by 4s to frame the rough opening for the windows. Add 4-by-4-by-30-inch angled corner braces to the rear bearing wall and the gable end walls.

continued »

GABLE DETAIL

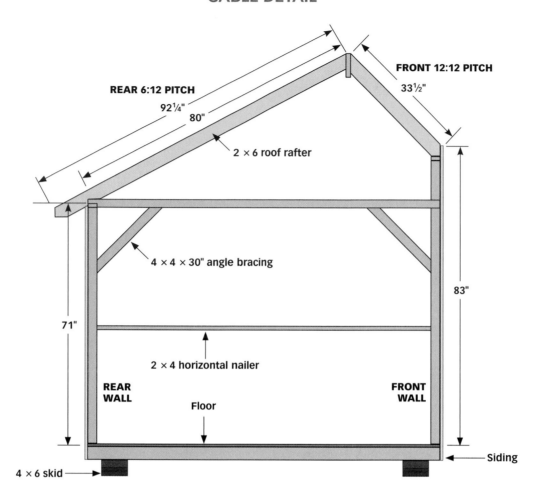

FRONT 12:12 PITCH

REAR 6:12 PITCH

92¼"

80"

33½"

2 × 6 roof rafter

4 × 4 × 30" angle bracing

83"

71"

2 × 4 horizontal nailer

REAR WALL

FRONT WALL

Floor

Siding

4 × 6 skid

7 INSTALL THE SIDING Choose siding that measures 1 by 6 or larger. Install the rear wall siding flush with the top plate; the rafter tails will fit over the siding. Nail the siding to the horizontal nailers, rim joists, and top plates. The siding will extend ¼ inch below the rim joist to ensure water drainage. Install the front wall siding allowing the siding to extend above the top plate a minimum of 3 inches. Wait to install the gable end wall siding, until after the roof is framed.

8 BUILD THE ROOF Frame the roof with a 1-by-8 ridge and 2-by-6 rafters 24 inches on center. Notch the rear rafters so that they sit on the top plate and tight against the siding. Cut a bird's-mouth notch in the front rafters so that they rest on the front top plate. Install 1-by-4 roof strapping 24 inches on center for attaching the metal roofing. When installing strapping, hold it back 2 inches from the ridge and make sure the last piece does not hang below the edge of the rafter. Install 1-by-6 collar ties tight to the ridge on all rafters except the ends. Install siding on the gable end walls. Install 1-by-12 bird blocking between the rafters and nail onto the top plate. Add 2-by-8 fascia to the gable ends and front wall and cut it flush with the rafter ends. Install 1-by-8 fascia on the rear wall. Add a second "shadow" fascia board using the same technique— 2 by 4 on the front and gable ends, and 1 by 4 on the rear wall. Note: If using asphalt shingles, sheath the roof with plywood instead of installing nailing straps (see page 78).

9 ADD TRIM, WINDOWS, AND DOORS Attach vertical 1-by-4 corner trim. Apply 1-by-3 stops to the inside of the window openings. Install the 1-by-5 doorjamb and the 1-by-4 exterior window and door trim. Build the set of double doors out of the siding material (see page 84). The secondary door of the set, or the one used less frequently, will need a foot latch at the bottom and a

BIRD BLOCK DETAIL

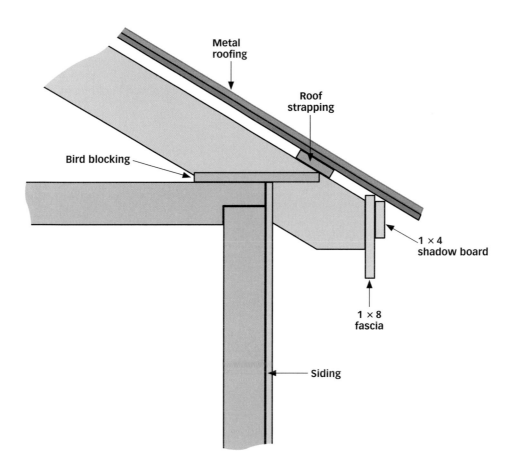

Metal roofing

Roof strapping

Bird blocking

1 × 4 shadow board

1 × 8 fascia

Siding

pull latch at the top. You may need to install a block on the secondary door to accept the latch. Install 1-by-2 door stops around the interior door frame and hang the doors. Install the barn sash windows hinged at the top and a 6-inch hook and two eye screws for each window. One eye screw is to hold the window in the open position, and the other is to lock it.

10 ADD WOOD VENTS AND BATTENS
Hold the wood vent in position, level it, and trace around the outside on the exterior of the building. Cut the siding and set the vent into the hole. Hold the vent tight to the top of the opening and screw it directly into the siding. Install trim around the vent to seal the gap. Install the battens over each seam in the siding with a pattern of two side-by-side nails in the same increments as the siding.

11 INSTALL THE METAL ROOFING
Attach the metal roofing to the roof strapping using 1½-inch roofing screws. The first sheet of metal should hang over the shadow fascia board by 2 inches on the gable ends and the front wall. Install all the roofing, cutting the last piece to fit, and then add the ridge cap. Be sure to follow the manufacturer's installation instructions for the metal roofing you choose.

12 FINAL DETAILS
After the roof is complete, you can remove the temporary bracing. Using treated 2-by-6 lumber, frame the entry ramp and add treated 5/4-by-6 decking (see page 94). Leave the first two decking boards off until you have attached the ramp to the shed's floor frame. Add interior details and exterior finishes.

SALTBOX SHED WITH WOOD STORAGE

Now that you're familiar with post-and-beam construction, you can easily expand on a simple shed plan to meet your specific storage needs. Build this 6-by-14-foot weekender shed using the same basic construction techniques as for the saltbox shed beginning on page 104. You are basically building one large structure with a partition down the middle, creating two separate storage spaces. The enclosed shed, measuring 6 by 7 feet, has a 5-foot-wide set of double doors and an entry ramp for storing large items like a garden tractor. The identically sized wood storage area has a framed opening in the front for easy access and can hold two cords of firewood. Adapt this shed design by adding windows, changing the door size, or using another roofing material.

Design by Jamaica Cottage Shop. To order plans for this project, see page 190.

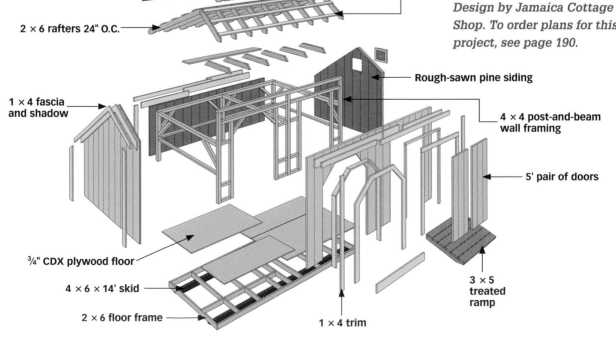

Corrugated metal roof

1 × 4 strapping

2 × 6 rafters 24" O.C.

1 × 4 fascia and shadow

Rough-sawn pine siding

4 × 4 post-and-beam wall framing

5' pair of doors

¾" CDX plywood floor

4 × 6 × 14' skid

3 × 5 treated ramp

2 × 6 floor frame

1 × 4 trim

GARDEN STORAGE SHED WITH METAL ROOF

Small in size but loaded with charm, this 4-by-8-foot shed is ideal for storing garden tools. Easily built on a foundation of precast concrete pavers, it features a corrugated metal roof at a 6:12 slope, recycled windows, and 1-by-6 fir siding. A simple barn door slides on an overhead track, and 1-by-6 fir flooring covers the 2-by-6 floor frame (see page 68). Small diamond-shaped windows in the gable ends add light to the interior and interest to the exterior. Simple 2-by-4 framed walls and rafters require no additional sheathing. The 5/4-by-4-inch trim is installed on top of the siding, and exposed nail heads add rustic detail.

Complete this picture with trim paint, your favorite garden ornament or birdhouse on the outside, and storage hooks and shelves on the inside, and you're ready to garden.

Design by Bob Bowling Rustics. For more information, see page 190.

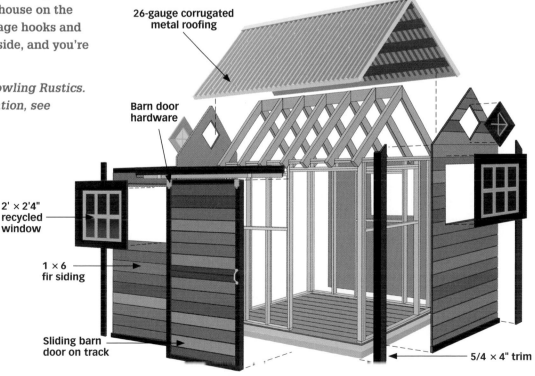

26-gauge corrugated metal roofing

Barn door hardware

2' × 2'4" recycled window

1 × 6 fir siding

Sliding barn door on track

5/4 × 4" trim

HIP ROOF SHED

This charming shed could be the focal point of your garden, especially if conveniently placed at the edge of a patio or amid garden beds. With a vine-covered arbor over the French doors, it could hold all of your gardening essentials as well as outdoor entertaining supplies while adding a beautiful structural element to your landscape.

MATERIALS LIST

Concrete, steel rebar, and steel mesh for slab foundation/floor

2 × 4 pressure-treated bottom plates

2 × 4 top plates, wall studs, sills, headers, trimmer studs, cripple studs

2 × 6 hip and jack rafters

2 awning-style windows with divided light, 1'6" × 3'

1 set of pre-hung divided-light French doors, 4' × 6'8"

1 × 4 trim

1 × 8 trim

5/4 × 4" fascia

½" CDX plywood sheathing for roof and walls

60-minute felt paper for roof and walls (drip edge)

Asphalt shingles and ridge cap

½ × 6 beveled cedar siding

Galvanized nails and outdoor screws

4 × 4 cedar for arbor brackets

2 × 8 cedar for arbor

2 × 2 cedar for trellis

1 × 2 cedar for trellis

2 × 4 cedar for trellis

Paint or stain

Design Details

Measuring 10 by 10 feet with two side windows and a pair of French doors for the entry, this shed plan calls for straightforward wall framing and a slab foundation. If the hip roof or the slab foundation is more than you want to tackle, consider hiring out those portions of the project (see page 74). Once the roof is framed, the sheathing and roofing will be easy to install. For the entry doors, consider obscure glass to block your view of the shed contents while allowing light inside. A small cupola, weather vane, or finial would look perfect as a finishing roof peak detail.

Design by Jean Zaputil. For more information, see page 190.

Building Tip: Smaller awning-style windows like the ones shown here are great for sheds and garages. You can leave them slightly open for ventilation without worrying about the occasional rain shower.

continued »

How to Build the Hip Roof Shed

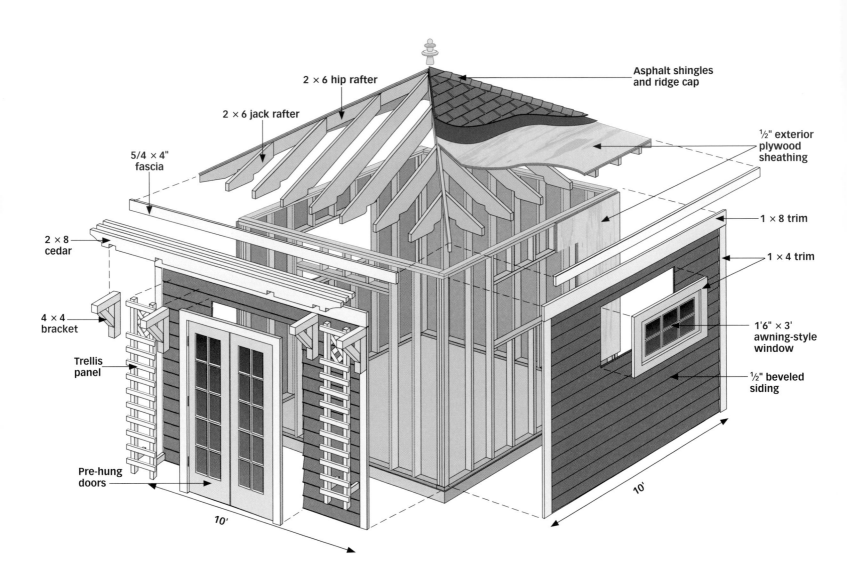

2 × 6 hip rafter

2 × 6 jack rafter

5/4 × 4" fascia

Asphalt shingles and ridge cap

½" exterior plywood sheathing

2 × 8 cedar

4 × 4 bracket

Trellis panel

Pre-hung doors

1 × 8 trim

1 × 4 trim

1'6" × 3' awning-style window

½" beveled siding

10'

10'

Building Tip: When framing a hip roof, run a string line above the center of each hip rafter before installing the jack rafters and use it as a reference point to ensure you are not knocking the hip rafter out of alignment.

ROOF DETAIL

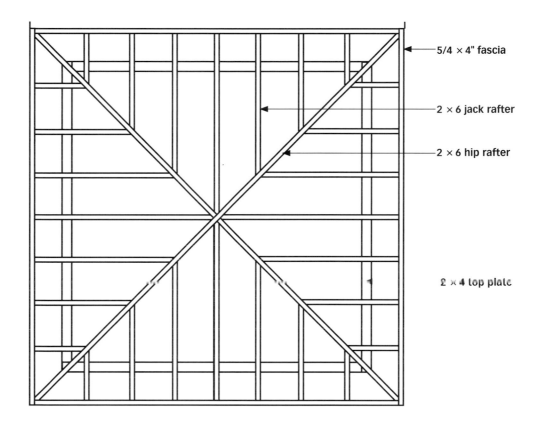

5/4 × 4" fascia

2 × 6 jack rafter

2 × 6 hip rafter

2 × 4 top plate

1 POUR THE FOUNDATION Excavate for the foundation on undisturbed, bearing soil. Form, reinforce, and pour the slab with anchor bolts and door openings in place (see pages 66–67).

2 FRAME THE ROOF To simplify the roof framing, build it on the floor of the shed before the walls are erected, carefully set it aside, and then move it into place when the wall framing is complete. This will require several strong helpers or the use of staging equipment. The roof pitch is 4:12. To frame the hip roof, cut a double set of top plates and temporarily attach one set along the foundation perimeter, drilling holes for the anchor bolts. Cut the four 2-by-6 hip rafters that run from each corner to the center. Install one pair of opposite hip rafters, then the other. Notch the rafters to fit over the top plates with a 12-inch overhang (see page 77). Check the angle cuts, fasten the hip rafters together, and temporarily screw them to the top plates. Install the jack rafters 16 inches on center. They will run at a 90-degree angle from the walls.

Note: If you are hiring someone to frame the hip roof, frame the walls first.

continued »

FRONT WALL DETAIL

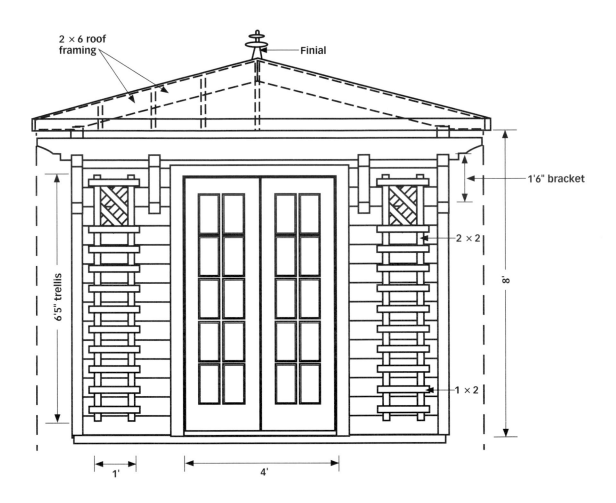

2 × 6 roof framing

Finial

1'6" bracket

6'5" trellis

2 × 2

1 × 2

8'

1'

4'

3 FRAME THE WALLS Use pressure-treated 2 by 4s for the mudsill. Transfer the anchor bolt locations and drill holes. Cut the top plates and lay out the walls using 2 by 4s 16 inches on center. Frame the rough openings for the windows and doors. Add trimmer studs, headers, cripple studs, and sills as required.

4 RAISE AND SECURE THE WALLS With help, raise each wall and secure it in place with anchor bolts. Brace the walls as needed. Check for plumb, level, and square. Screw the walls together and tighten the connectors. Install the previously cut top plate.

5 ADD THE ROOF With several strong helpers, lift the framed roof into place and secure it to the walls by screwing down through the attached top plate. Cut the rafter tails off at a right angle to create a flat soffit and attachment space for the fascia. Install the 5/4-by-4-inch fascia board. Sheath the roof with plywood, roofing felt, and asphalt shingles and then add the ridge caps (see pages 78–79).

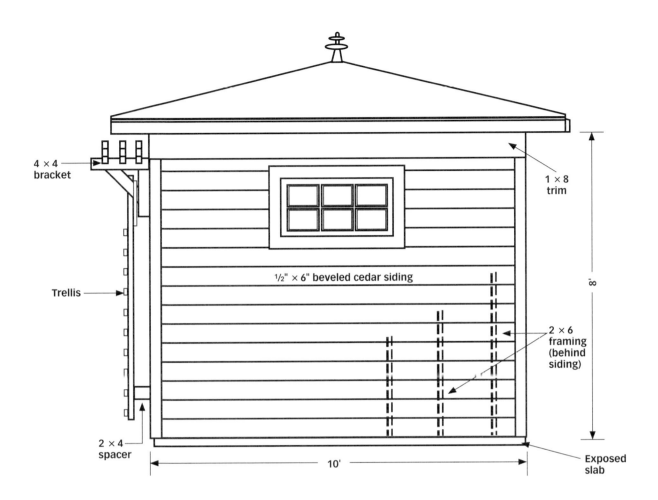

4 × 4 bracket

1 × 8 trim

Trellis

½" × 6" beveled cedar siding

2 × 6 framing (behind siding)

8'

2 × 4 spacer

10'

Exposed slab

6 ADD SHEATHING, SIDING, AND TRIM
Sheath the walls with ½-inch CDX plywood and a layer of 60-minute felt paper. Because you are using beveled siding, you will need to install the windows, pre-hung entry door, and trim before the siding, making sure the trim pieces are slightly thicker than the installed siding. Build the 4-by-4 arbor brackets and install them before the siding so they sit flat against the wall. Enclose the underside of the soffit with exterior-grade plywood.

Building Tip: It's much easier to paint or stain the arbor and trellis panels before installing them.

7 ADD THE TRELLIS PANELS AND ARBOR
Build the trellis panels out of 2-by-2 and 1-by-2 cedar as shown. Attach them to the shed's exterior using pieces of 2-by-4 cedar as spacers. The trellis panels should sit 5 inches from the siding. You will need to cut the angle of the siding on the end of the spacer, pre-drill it, and attach it gently with screws so you don't split the siding. Cut the 2-by-8 arbor pieces as shown, using a jigsaw to make the curved end cuts (see page 43). Mark the four bracket locations on the bottom of each 2 by 8 and cut 1½-inch-deep notches so the arbor pieces sit down over the brackets. Attach them with outdoor screws.

CHICKEN COOP SHED

The owners of some lucky city chickens wanted a classy coop that would look good near their contemporary home. With the house's architectural style as inspiration, this sophisticated and highly functional design met all their needs. As a bonus, the coop can be converted easily to a convenient storage shed. The entry, with a single-light French door and a concrete floor, gives the owners easy access and the chickens a great view, and it lets light into the coop. A raised portion of the floor allows the chicken run to extend below the coop and could be replaced easily with additional flooring and siding to make the entire structure full height. The windows are screened with ¼-inch hardware cloth to keep out potential egg thieves and to open the enclosure for ventilation in warm weather.

A metal shed roof, beveled horizontal siding, both fixed and operable windows made from twin-wall polycarbonate panels, plenty of electrical receptacles, and heavy-duty light fixtures make this a beautiful and hardworking addition to a small yard.

Design by Jean Zaputil. For more information, see page 190.

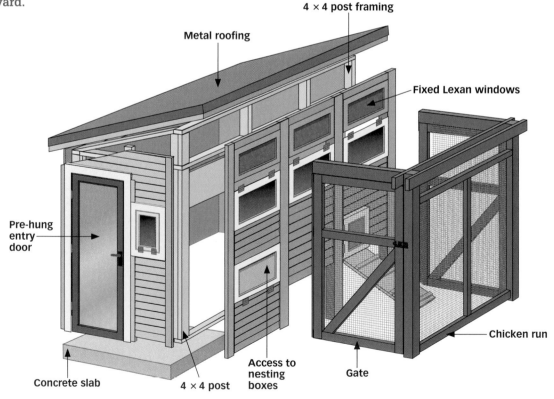

4 × 4 post framing

Metal roofing

Fixed Lexan windows

Pre-hung entry door

Concrete slab

4 × 4 post

Access to nesting boxes

Gate

Chicken run

PLAYHOUSE WITH FRONT PORCH AND SHUTTERS

This child's playhouse is a dream come true. Easily built on a temporary foundation, the 8-by-8-foot child-size structure gets its charm from its many architectural details.

Treated 4-by-4 runners form the base for the 2-by-4 framed plywood floor. The floor then makes an ideal spot to frame the walls. This tiny house provides you with the opportunity to frame a gable roof with dormer. A dormer with fan-shaped plywood appliqué highlights the front porch entry. The windows, hinged to swing open and made of plexiglass, are complete with window boxes, perfect for the budding gardener. Shutters, gable-end wood vents with screens, cement-board siding, and an asphalt shingle roof make this a house your child will be glad to call home.

This playhouse could easily be adapted to match your home's style with a change in details like shutters, roofing, or siding.

Design by HDA, Inc.
To order plans for this project, see page 168.

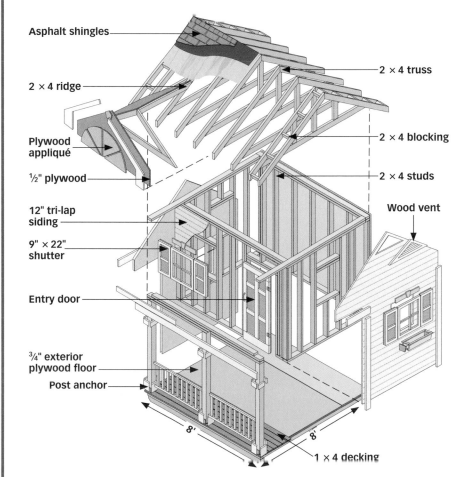

Asphalt shingles

2 × 4 ridge

Plywood appliqué

½" plywood

12" tri-lap siding

9" × 22" shutter

Entry door

¾" exterior plywood floor

Post anchor

2 × 4 truss

2 × 4 blocking

2 × 4 studs

Wood vent

8'

8'

1 × 4 decking

Attention to detail and an innovative approach to using basic building materials turn a simple 12-by-12-foot shed into a garden jewel. Simply framed using 2-by-4 construction, this shed is built on a base of 4-by-4 skids with pressure-treated 2-by-6 floor framing. It features a hip roof with cupola, a single French entry door, seven custom-built awning-style windows, and a cedar shake roof. The entire shed is sheathed in beveled siding. An additional layer of cedar shakes with a beveled cap is applied to each corner, giving a graceful flare to the overall shape of the structure. Mitered moldings with flashing and a sill add architectural detail to each window. Exposed rafter tails create a subtle pattern that wraps the perimeter of the square hip roof. The roof is framed to accept the generous 2-by-2-foot cupola, complete with screened ventilation holes, stone tile appliqués, its own hip roof and exposed rafter tails, and a wood finial. Vintage-style lanterns light the entry, a yellow pine floor adds warmth to the interior, and the rest of the details are up to you.

Design by Artisan Sheds. To order plans for this project, see page 190.

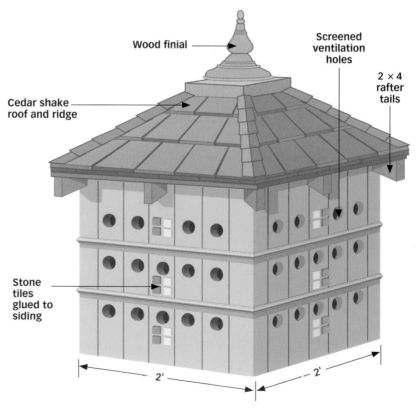

Wood finial

Screened ventilation holes

Cedar shake roof and ridge

2 × 4 rafter tails

Stone tiles glued to siding

2'   2'

GARDEN SHED WITH ARCHITECTURAL SALVAGE

Thinking of Using Architectural Salvage?

If you already have items you want to use, that's great. If not, find them first. Then design your shed or garage around those reclaimed products.

Salvaged parts you might consider using for a shed:

- Doors
- Windows
- Trim or molding
- Shutters
- Light fixtures
- Stained glass
- Door or window hardware
- Storage units or cabinets
- Shelf brackets
- Tool racks
- Flooring
- Almost anything!

An unused space between two raised garden beds seemed tailor-made for a small storage shed in this city garden. Measuring just 6 by 6 feet, this structure holds a lawn mower, a rack of tools, and shelves for gardening supplies. It features a vintage window and a pair of French doors salvaged from a home remodel. Easy to build, this shed was framed with 2 by 4s on a foundation made of treated timbers. The back peak of the shed, which sits against the fence line, rises to 8 feet, 6 inches high, allowing for a 4:12 slope, just enough for asphalt shingles. The salvaged doors, which are standard height and 4 feet wide as a pair, required the building of top and side jambs before installation. The patina created by years of paint layers provided just the right contrast to the beveled cedar siding and trim.

Design by Jean Zaputil. For more information, see page 190.

BUTTERFLY ROOF SHED

Simple in form but unique in its design details, this 10-by-12-foot contemporary shed makes an inviting studio, home office, guest house, or weekend escape. The butterfly roof is a focal point in any landscape. A pair of single-light French entry doors and three operable awning-style windows let in ample sunlight. Customize this shed by using alternative siding—horizontal, vertical, or metal. Insulate the walls, ceiling, and floor and add systems for comfortable use year-round.

MATERIALS LIST

Concrete deck blocks

2 × 8, 2 × 10 pressure-treated floor and roof framing

2 × 6 wall framing, window headers

Joist hangers

2 × 10 window and door headers

½" exterior-grade plywood subfloor and roof framing

Self-adhering deck protector wrap

Metal roofing with pre-finished aluminum drip edge

Ice and water shield

⅛:12 slope custom pre-finished aluminum gutter with rain chain

2 metal awning-style windows to fit RO size 2'6" by 1'6"

1 metal awning-style window to fit RO size 2'6" by 2'6"

1 pair of metal or wood single-light French doors 5' wide by 6'8" high

Peel-and-stick flashing for window, door, and siding

Cement board panels

Cement board soffit panels

Stainless-steel screws

Roof rafter ties

OPTIONAL

R15 batt insulation for walls

R30 batt insulation for ceiling

Rigid insulation for between floor joists

Vapor barrier

Design Details

Set on concrete deck blocks, the platform for this shed is framed with pressure-treated lumber and finished with a plywood subfloor. The 2-by-6 walls are framed in modular sections, raised onto the floor platform, and sheathed in plywood. A layer of building paper followed by the installation of prefabricated plastic battens creates a drainage plane between the sheathing and the cement board siding panels (also known as rain screen construction). The inverted metal-clad roof slopes to a central custom-fabricated gutter that carries water off the back of the building and down a rain chain.

Design by NeoShed. To order plans or a kit for this project, see page 190.

Building Tip: Use extra care when handling fiber cement board, as it can break easily before it is attached to your structure.

continued »

How to Build the Butterfly Roof Shed

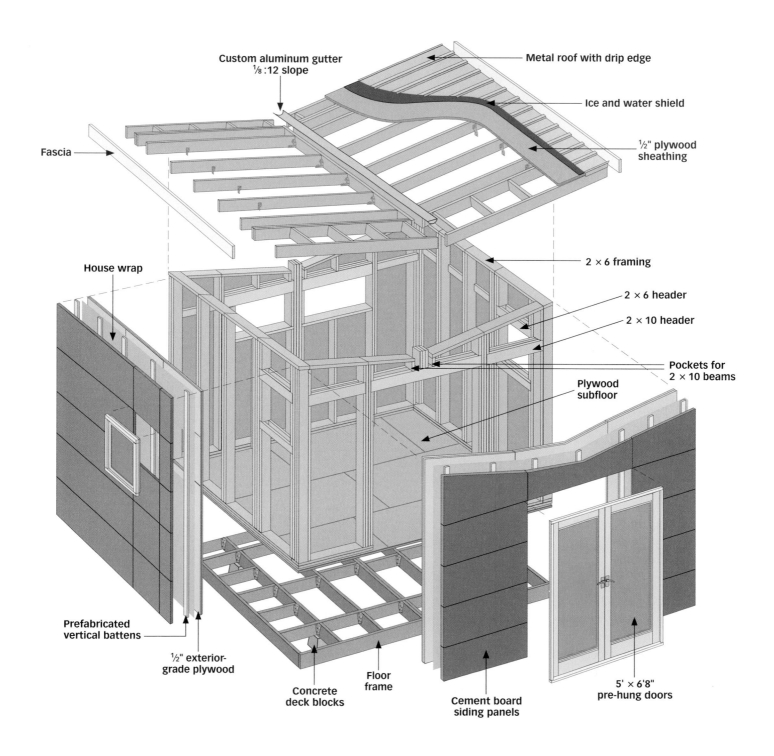

Custom aluminum gutter ⅛ :12 slope

Metal roof with drip edge

Ice and water shield

½" plywood sheathing

Fascia

House wrap

2 × 6 framing

2 × 6 header

2 × 10 header

Pockets for 2 × 10 beams

Plywood subfloor

Prefabricated vertical battens

½" exterior-grade plywood

Concrete deck blocks

Floor frame

Cement board siding panels

5' × 6'8" pre-hung doors

SUBFRAME

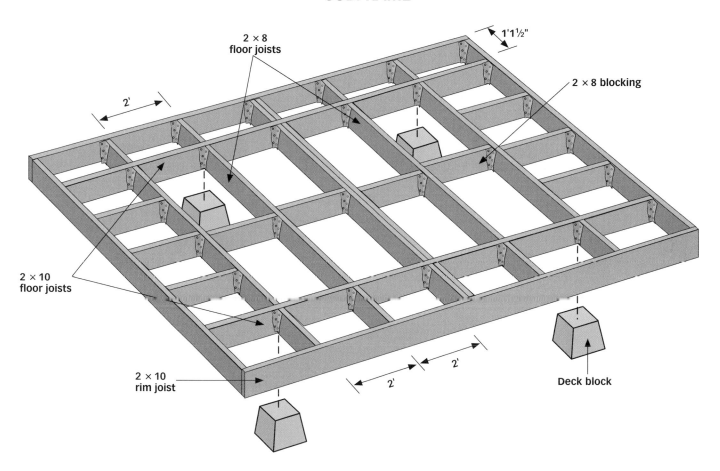

2 × 8 floor joists

1'1½"

2 × 8 blocking

2'

2 × 10 floor joists

2 × 10 rim joist

2'

2'

Deck block

1 **BUILD THE FLOOR** Install the deck blocks on compacted crushed rock. Place the 2-by-10 joists onto the deck blocks and level them. Attach the 2-by-10 rim joists to the beams and check for square. Using metal joist hangers, attach the 2-by-8 floor joists to the beams and rim joists and keep checking for square and level. Add 2-by-8 blocking to the center of each joist span, then install the plywood subfloor (see pages 68–69). If you are insulating your shed, add a layer of vapor barrier below the subfloor and rigid insulation panels between the floor joists. Choose the thickness based on your required R-value.

Building Tip: Plan for any electrical and plumbing systems and install them as needed before finishing the floor platform.

continued »

WALL SECTIONS—ALL FRAMING 2 × 6

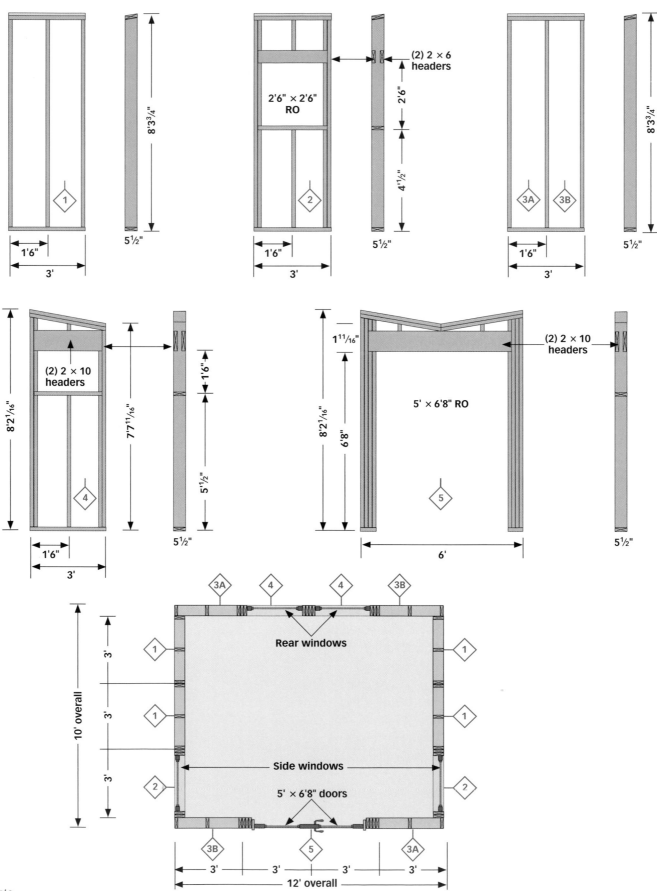

8'3¾"

1

5½"

1'6"

3'

2'6" × 2'6" RO

(2) 2 × 6 headers

2'6"

4'1½"

2

5½"

1'6"

3'

8'3¾"

3A 3B

5½"

1'6"

3'

(2) 2 × 10 headers

8'2¹⁄₁₆"

7'7¹¹⁄₁₆"

1'6"

5'1½"

4

5½"

1'6"

3'

1¹¹⁄₁₆"

(2) 2 × 10 headers

8'2¹⁄₁₆"

6'8"

5' × 6'8" RO

5

5½"

6'

3A 4 4 3B

Rear windows

1 1

10' overall

3'

3'

3'

1 1

2 Side windows 2

5' × 6'8" doors

3B 5 3A

3' 3' 3' 3'

12' overall

2 FRAME AND SHEATH THE WALLS

Install the bottom plate on the floor platform, removing the rough opening for the doors. Five different wall panels form the walls of the shed. Label the bottom plate indicating the location of each wall section. Using the plan, build each wall section and frame for windows and doors and label them. Raise the walls, brace and plumb each panel, and attach them to the bottom plate with screws 6 inches on center. Once the panels are anchored, use screws 12 inches on center to connect them. Keep checking for plumb and square. Attach the top plates and sheath the panels in ½-inch exterior-grade plywood. Note: You may sheath the panels in plywood before installing them on the bottom plate. See wall elevations at left.

3 FRAME AND SHEATH THE ROOF

Set the 2-by-10 roof beams into the pockets formed by the wall panels. Check for level. Start from the center and attach the rafters to the beams 24 inches on center. Build and attach the outriggers to the two outer rafters with screws 6 inches on center and staggered. Install the fascia board on all four sides. Starting from the valley edge of the rafters, attach the roof sheathing with screws 6 inches on center, making sure the screws penetrate the rafters (see pages 76–79).

Building Tip: Be sure to install an insect barrier (screen) at the bottom of the wall assembly and in any gaps to prevent insects from nesting in your rain screen siding.

4 INSTALL THE ROOF AND GUTTER

Lay continuous strips of peel-and-stick flashing along the bottom edge of the sheathing on both sides of the gutter valley. Place gutter into the roof void and check for correct slope. Attach the gutter flange to the sheathing using screws and pre-drilled holes. Lay a strip of peel-and-stick flashing across the flange and another strip 3 inches away overlapping the first strip. Install the ice and water shield underlayment and then the metal roofing, following the manufacturer's instructions and using specified hardware. Install the pre-finished aluminum drip edge. Hang the rain chain under the gutter opening at the back of the shed.

5 ADD SIDING, WINDOWS, AND DOORS

Attach house wrap to the exterior sheathing using a staple gun or cap stapler. Wrap all rough openings (see pages 82–86). Seal all seams and tears with house-wrap tape. Install the pre-hung doors and windows and install flashing per the manufacturer's instructions. Install prefabricated vertical battens or other furring strips, screwing them onto the exterior sheathing and using the same spacing as the wall studs. Following the manufacturer's instructions, cut cement board siding into panels as shown, then pre-drill and attach over the plastic battens using stainless-steel screws. Maintain the same screw head pattern for each panel and take care not to over-tighten the screws. Caulk and seal the perimeter of the doors and windows. Enclose the soffits using cement board soffit planks.

6 FINISHING

If you are insulating your structure, finalize all necessary wiring and plumbing before adding the batt insulation. Make sure all inspections have been completed before installing the interior wall sheathing, trim, fixtures, and any other details.

BACKYARD STUDIO

Longing to expand your studio or work space but unwilling to take on an expensive remodel or addition? Need a work area that's separate from your living quarters? Consider adding a fully finished and insulated studio shed to your yard. Smart building practices and energy-efficient materials make this contemporary shed a hard-working and fully functional space. Built on either a framed floor system or a concrete slab and flooded with light from horizontal clerestory windows, it features a shed roof with generous eaves supported by 2-by-8 tapered rafters. Denim insulation, double-pane low-E windows, Zip-System waterproof wall panels, and a corrugated steel roof with exposed fasteners add up to a shed that's smarter, if not necessarily bigger. Finish details include brushed aluminum trim and hardware, pre-finished hardwood flooring, walls of either gypsum wall board or birch paneling, and interior lighting.

Designs by Studio Shed. To order any of these shed kits, see page 190.

GREENHOUSE SHED

This versatile, light-filled structure could serve many functions—greenhouse, potting shed, workshop, or studio—or multiple purposes at once. Clear glazed greenhouse window panels and a French entry door let the light stream in. Choose the site for this shed carefully depending on how much direct light and heat you want.

MATERIALS LIST

4 × 4 pressure-treated foundation runners

2 × 4 pressure-treated floor framing

5/4 × 6" pressure-treated floor decking

2 × 6 pressure-treated ramp

2 × 4 wall studs, plates, collar ties

2 × 6 wall headers, rafters, blocking

2 × 8 plant shelf, ridge board

½" exterior plywood roof sheathing

⅜" exterior plywood soffits

15-light pre-hung French entry door

10:12, 4' base wood louvers with screen

1 × 1 window frames

¼" plexiglass windows, cut to fit

1 × 2, 1 × 3, 1 × 4, 1 × 6 window and door trim, corner trim

1 × 8 fascia

15# roofing felt

12" tri-lap cement board siding

Silicone

Exterior paint, stain, or sealer

Cement-coated nails

Galvanized nails and screws

Roofing nails

T-type metal wall bracing

Design Details

This 10-by-10-foot greenhouse shed may be built on a temporary foundation of treated 4-by-4 runners, or you can opt for a more permanent slab or concrete footing foundation (see page 63). The roof is framed like a saltbox structure with asymmetrical rafter lengths and side wall heights. Wood louvers on the gable ends provide the option of added ventilation. The window panels are made of 1-by-1-inch framing and clear plexiglass. To customize this structure, you may choose alternative siding, door style, operable side windows, or roof material. Be sure to plan for electrical and plumbing needs before you build (see page 88).

Design by HDA, Inc. To order plans for this project, see page 160.

Building Tip: To prevent accidents, keep your work area clean of debris and tools that are not being used.

continued »

How to Build the Greenhouse Shed

1 **PREPARE THE SITE AND BUILD THE FOUNDATION** Select a level location slightly larger than the footprint of the shed. Dig four trenches 8 inches wide and 11 feet long for the 4-by-4 runners and install them, checking for square. The diagonal measurement should equal 14 feet 1¾ inches (see page 62).

2 **FRAME THE FLOOR** Use two treated 2 by 4s that are each 10 feet long for the band boards, then cut 11 treated floor joists 9 feet 9 inches long to frame the floor (see page 69). Position the floor frame onto the runners and check for level and square. Toenail the 2-by-4 joists into the runners using 16d cc nails. Install 5/4-by-6-inch treated decking on the floor frame.

3 **FRAME THE WALLS** Use the deck as a work surface to frame the walls. Since each wall of the greenhouse shed is slightly different, consult the plan and carefully cut 2-by-4 studs and plates for each wall, the 2-by-6 door header, and the 2-by-8 plant shelf. Wall studs are 16 inches on center. Door and wood vent sizes may vary by manufacturer, so verify rough opening sizes prior to framing. Assemble the walls (see pages 70–73).

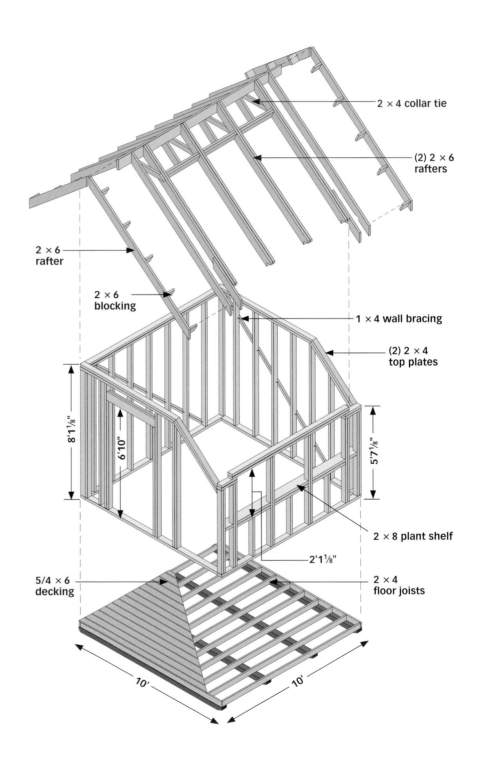

2 × 4 collar tie

(2) 2 × 6 rafters

2 × 6 rafter

2 × 6 blocking

1 × 4 wall bracing

(2) 2 × 4 top plates

8'1⅛"

6'10"

5'7⅛"

2 × 8 plant shelf

2'1⅛"

5/4 × 6 decking

2 × 4 floor joists

10'

10'

ROOF FRAMING PLAN

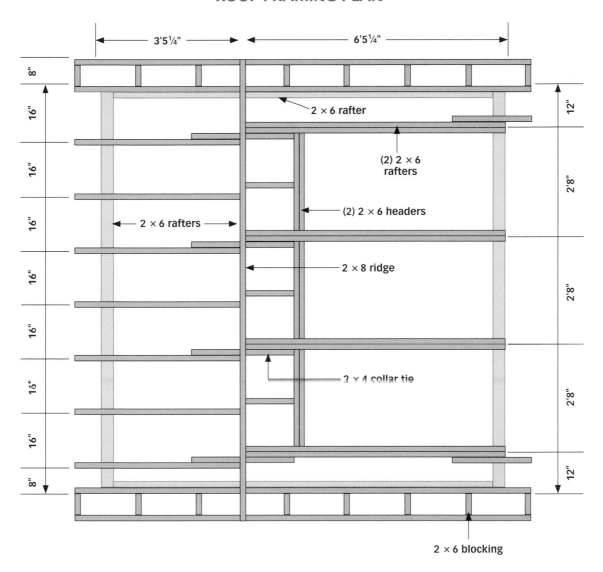

3'5¼"　　　　6'5¼"

8"

16"

16"

16"

16"

16"

16"

8"

12"

2'8"

2'8"

2'8"

12"

2 × 6 rafter

(2) 2 × 6 rafters

(2) 2 × 6 headers

2 × 6 rafters

2 × 8 ridge

2 × 4 collar tie

2 × 6 blocking

4 RAISE THE WALLS Position the walls on the deck floor as shown and install temporary bracing as necessary (see page 72). Make sure the walls are plumb and square and secure the wall panels to the floor. Connect the panels at the corners (see page 73) and install the 2-by-8 plant shelf.

5 FRAME AND SHEATH THE ROOF Using the framing plan, cut the 2-by-8 ridge board 11 feet 4 inches long and set it in place using temporary bracing (see page 76). Mark the top plates on the left and right walls for the location of the rafters. Cut one of each size rafter per plan with a bird's mouth cut to fit over the top plate as necessary (see page 77). Check each rafter for fit and use them as templates to cut the remaining pieces. Assemble the roof as shown, cutting 2-by-4 collar ties and additional rafters per the plan.

Measure and cut ½-inch exterior plywood for roof sheathing, allowing a ¾-inch overhang at all edges of the roof to cover the 1-by-8 fascia. Hold the plywood back 1½ inches, exposing the inside 2-by-6 rafter around the window opening for the plexiglass to rest on.

continued »

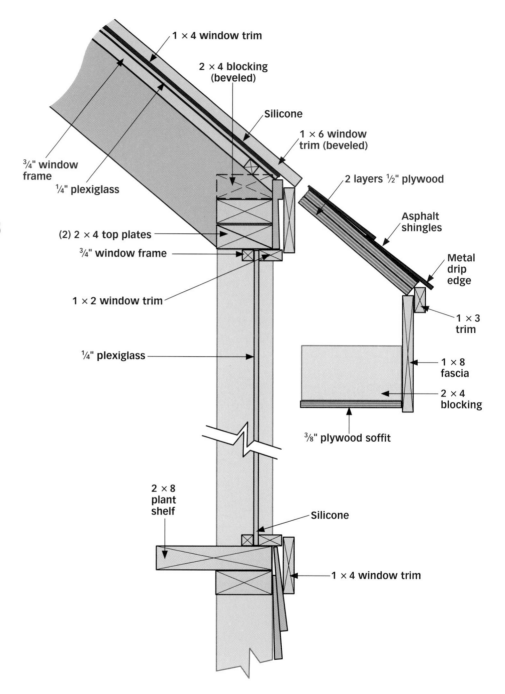

1 × 4 window trim

2 × 4 blocking (beveled)

Silicone

1 × 6 window trim (beveled)

2 layers ½" plywood

Asphalt shingles

Metal drip edge

¾" window frame

¼" plexiglass

(2) 2 × 4 top plates

¾" window frame

1 × 2 window trim

¼" plexiglass

1 × 3 trim

1 × 8 fascia

2 × 4 blocking

⅜" plywood soffit

2 × 8 plant shelf

Silicone

1 × 4 window trim

6 FRAME THE WINDOWS

Glue and screw ¾-inch window frames together with 1½-inch galvanized screws to support the plexiglass. Set the frames in place flush with the top of the rafters at the roof and 1⅛ inch in from the outside of the front and right wall. Pre-drill holes and screw the ¾-inch frames in place. Cut the ¼-inch plexiglass to fit the window openings. Run a bead of clear silicone around the exposed 2-by-6 rafter and set the plexiglass in place on the roof. Run a second bead of silicone along the outside perimeter of the glass. Apply 1-by-4 and 1-by-6 window trim to the roof, pre-drilling the holes through the plexiglass and trim to avoid splitting. Apply a bead of silicone at the corners where the plexiglass and trim meet. Insert plexiglass windows at the front and right walls and apply silicone to the perimeter before installing 1-by-2 trim.

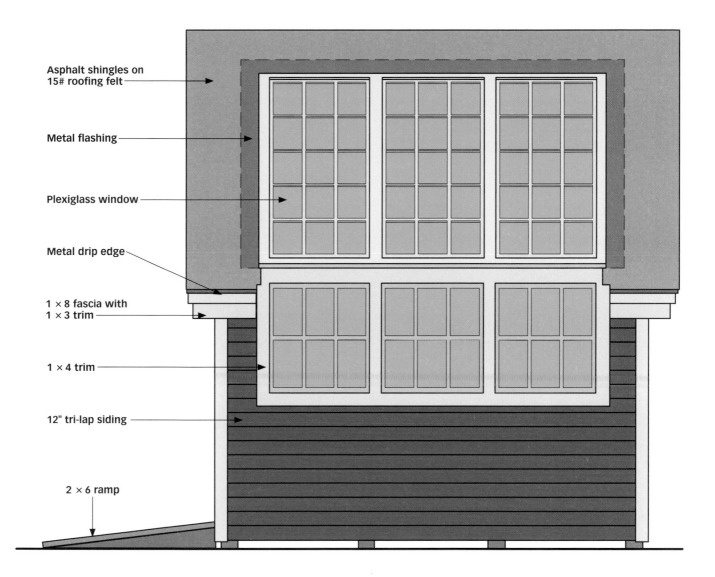

Asphalt shingles on
15# roofing felt

Metal flashing

Plexiglass window

Metal drip edge

1 × 8 fascia with
1 × 3 trim

1 × 4 trim

12" tri-lap siding

2 × 6 ramp

7 FINISH THE ROOF Apply a second layer of ½-inch plywood to the entire right side of the roof (the side with windows) to make the surface flush with the 1-by-4 trim. Add metal flashing to the window trim. Apply 1-by-8 fascia board and 1-by-3 trim. Add 15# roofing felt with ⅞-inch roofing nails (see page 78). Install 2-by-4 blocking at each rafter location to frame the soffits and then apply ⅜-inch plywood to the underside.

8 SIDING AND FINAL DETAILS Install corner trim. Apply 12-inch tri-lap cement board siding for each wall starting 2 inches up from the bottom of the runners. Install wood vents per the manufacturer's instructions and then trim with 1 by 4. Install the entry door and trim. Build the entry ramp using treated 2-by-6 lumber for the frame and 5/4-by-6 decking (see page 94). Apply exterior finishes.

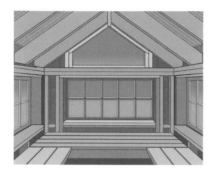

A wonderful addition to any garden, this 6-by-8-foot greenhouse is pleasing to look at, enjoyable to work in, and highly functional. Build this greenhouse using post-and-beam construction techniques (see page 104) or easily frame it using standard 2-by-4 wall framing (see page 70). A combination front door and five barn sash windows allow light to penetrate the interior without causing overheating. The roof is translucent corrugated fiberglass over rafters and roof strapping. Build the foundation from pressure-treated 4-by-6 skids (see page 62) and then add the floor of your choice—brick, stone, or gravel. A wraparound workbench sits just below the windowsill to accommodate trays of seedlings or overwintering plants. Customize your greenhouse by adding features like the narrow window next to the front door (shown here) or your own hand-built door.

Design by Jamaica Cottage Shop. To order plans for this project, see page 190.

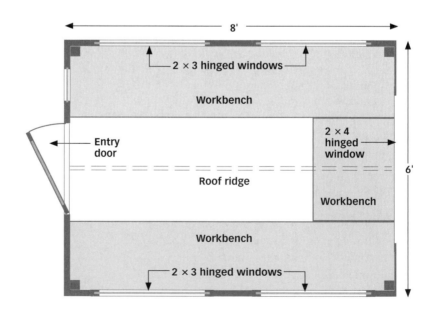

HOBBY GREENHOUSE

This roomy 12-by-12-foot shed and greenhouse can be downsized easily for a smaller garden. Eliminate the 4 feet to the left of the door for an 8-by-12-foot shed or the two rear skylight panels for an 8-by-8-foot shed. Built of western red cedar with thermoplastic panels (Lexan) that transmit 90 percent of the light while blocking UV rays, this hobby greenhouse can double as a light-filled studio or workshop. The Dutch door and operable rear window let fresh air in while you work. Skylight panels slide under the edge of the wood roof shingles and are first attached to the rafters with foam tape. A pre-drilled wood roof strip covers the seam and attaches with 2-inch screws and neoprene washers. The bottom edge of the plastic panels overhangs the rafters by 2 inches.

Design by Cedarshed. To order plans for this project, see page 190.

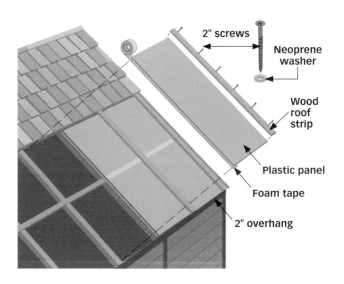

2" screws

Neoprene washer

Wood roof strip

Plastic panel

Foam tape

2" overhang

CRAFTSMAN GARAGE

This one-car Craftsman-style garage was designed to blend seamlessly with the adjacent house and be a focal point in the owner's backyard garden. It features a stepped perimeter wall foundation to accommodate the sloping yard, allowing soil to be backfilled against the foundation on three sides. This design could easily be adapted to a level site by eliminating the foundation steps. Because two walls of this garage are close to property lines, building code requires them to be one-hour fire walls. Check your local building code for requirements.

MATERIALS LIST

Concrete, anchor bolts, straps, and drainage

2 × 4 #2 DF studs for wall framing and top plate

2 × 8 #2 DF ridge board

2 × 6 #2 DF rafters

½" CDX plywood sheathing for walls and roof

60-minute felt paper for sheathing walls and roof–drip edge

2 × 4 pressure-treated mudsill

2 × 8 #2 DF collar ties

#1 red cedar shingles for siding

5/4 × 8" pre-primed fascia

Continuous ridge vent for roof

Asphalt shingles and ridge cap

4' × 1'4" awning-style wood windows, two units mulled together

3' × 6'8" entrance door

9'10" × 7' carriage house–style garage door with opener

⅝" fire-rated gypsum drywall

Gutters and downspouts

Interior trim

3 porch lights, photo cell/motion sensor

Galvanized nails and outdoor screws

Door threshold and hardware

Electrical supplies: conduit, switches, interior fixtures

Flashing

Design Details

Craftsman details that give this garage its character include custom wood awning-style windows (joined at the factory), a wood carriage house door, window and door trim that matches the vintage trim on the home, aged copper craftsman light fixtures, beadboard trim enclosing the soffits, and premium red cedar shingle siding. But the basic structure of this garage allows you to change its style easily. You may opt for alternative doors and windows, siding, roof material, trim, or fixtures, or add a feature like an arbor, trellis, or rooftop cupola. Here, the builder incorporated porch lights controlled by a photo cell and a motion sensor to provide safe entrance after dark. With the stepped foundation, the door entrances can remain at the patio level and the stone retaining wall can be built against the garage foundation, creating an upper tier of garden space and allowing mature trees to remain in place.

Design by Jean Zaputil. For more information, see page 190.

continued »

How to Build the Craftsman Garage

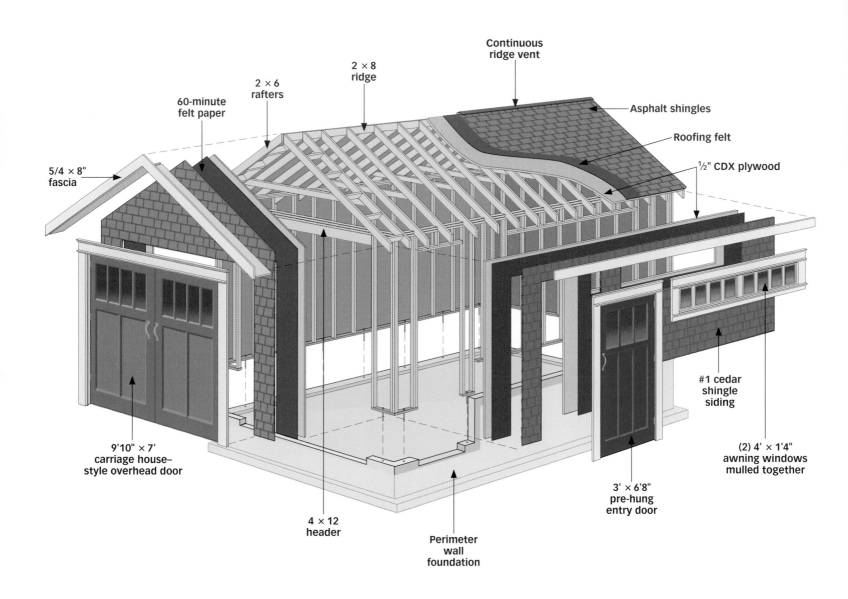

Continuous ridge vent

2 × 8 ridge

2 × 6 rafters

60-minute felt paper

Asphalt shingles

Roofing felt

5/4 × 8" fascia

½" CDX plywood

#1 cedar shingle siding

9'10" × 7' carriage house–style overhead door

(2) 4' × 1'4" awning windows mulled together

4 × 12 header

3' × 6'8" pre-hung entry door

Perimeter wall foundation

FOOTING DETAIL

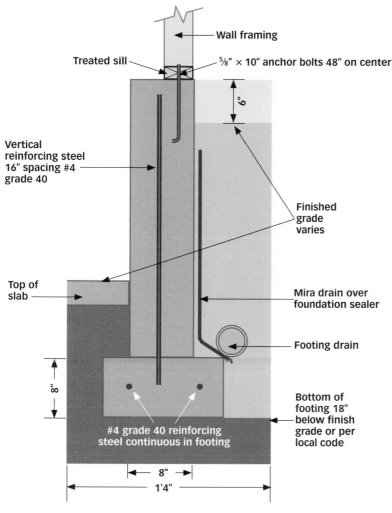

Wall framing

Treated sill

⅝" × 10" anchor bolts 48" on center

6"

Vertical reinforcing steel 16" spacing #4 grade 40

Finished grade varies

Top of slab

Mira drain over foundation sealer

Footing drain

8"

Bottom of footing 18" below finish grade or per local code

#4 grade 40 reinforcing steel continuous in footing

8"

1'4"

1 FORM AND POUR THE FOUNDATION AND FLOOR

The perimeter wall foundation is formed and poured with anchors, straps, and door openings in place. Sealer is applied to the ground contact area of the foundation wall, and drainage is installed. Electrical conduit is run to the structure as necessary. After the walls are stripped and cured, the concrete floor, reinforced with wire mesh, can be poured between the foundation walls (with slope for drainage to the front). See pages 63–67 for information on foundations and how to pour a concrete slab. You may wish to have a professional do this step.

PLAN

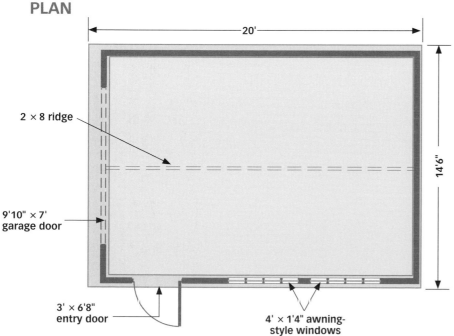

20'

2 × 8 ridge

14'6"

9'10" × 7' garage door

3' × 6'8" entry door

4' × 1'4" awning-style windows

2 FRAME THE WALLS

Use pressure-treated 2 by 4s for the mudsill. Transfer anchor bolt locations and drill holes. Align strap locations with wall studs. Cut top plates to match mudsills and lay out wall studs 16 inches on center. If the foundation steps up, adjust the walls accordingly to achieve equal height. Lay out rough openings for doors and windows. Build the walls in sections. Add trimmer studs, headers, cripple studs, and sills as required.

continued »

3 RAISE THE WALLS Starting with the side walls, place each wall section over the anchor bolts, slip on washers and nuts, then hand tighten. Brace each wall as necessary. Check for plumb, level, and square. Screw the walls together adding corner blocks and tighten connectors. Install double top plates and mark rafter locations 16 inches on center.

4 FRAME THE ROOF Using a 5:12 slope, make a rafter template with a bird's-mouth cut. Note that the overhangs are 4 inches on three sides and 12 inches in the front. Install the ridge beam, rafters, rafter clips, and rake in the front. Install 2-by-8 collar ties on the bottom third of every other rafter.

5 INSTALL ROOFING MATERIAL Sheath the roof with ½-inch CDX plywood and roofing felt. Install 5/4-by-8-inch fascia on all sides. Install the continuous roof vent, asphalt shingles, and drip edge.

6 ADD THE SIDING AND TRIM Sheath the walls with ½-inch CDX plywood, then add a layer of 60-minute felt paper. Because you are using cedar shingles for siding, you'll need to install the windows, pre-hung entry door, and window or door trim before shingling, making sure the trim is thicker than the installed shingles. Add flashing on the top edge of the trim. Electrical lines should be run at this stage of construction. Add wood mounting plates in the location of the outdoor fixtures along with the trim.

7 INSTALL FINISHES Install interior finishes, including the interior gypsum drywall required for the one-hour firewalls. Make sure final electrical work is done, including a receptacle for the garage door opener. You may wish to have the garage door manufacturer handle its installation. As a final step, add gutters, primer, and exterior paint.

Building Tip: During the roofing phase of your project, know your physical limitations. If you're uncomfortable with heights or feel unstable on a ladder, call a professional.

FRENCH DOOR GARAGE

There's more than one way to think about a garage. Yes, it's a place to park your car, but it could also be a place to entertain. When it came time to replace a tiny one-car garage in this small backyard, space considerations and building code limitations necessitated that the garage be attached to the existing Dutch Colonial home. To architecturally connect the garage to the home and garden, a pair of French doors with sidelights and a single French entry door were ordered pre-hung as one unit and added to the wall facing the patio. Obscure glass blocks the view of the car inside. If the homeowners decide to have a party, they move the car out, open the doors to the finished interior, and gain considerable entertaining space. A wooden carriage house garage door, copper fixtures, a mortared stone landing, and a wood shingle exterior make this garage a true extension of the home.

Design by Jean Zaputil. For more information, see page 190.

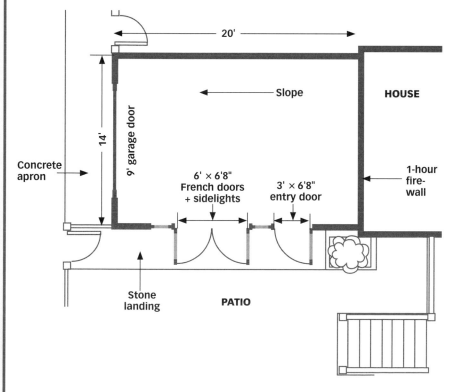

STORAGE BARN

A contemporary take on a classic structure, this 12-by-22-foot barn offers plenty of storage space for garden tools and large equipment like riding lawn mowers. An oversized, functional cupola adds light and ventilation to the interior, and hard-working materials make this a rugged structure. You can easily adapt the design and function of this barn by changing the window sizes, siding, fixtures, or style of door.

MATERIALS LIST

Concrete, anchor bolts, reinforcing steel and mesh, forming materials for foundation

Pressure-treated 2 × 4s for sole plate

2 × 4s for wall framing, cupola rafters

½" exterior plywood for wall, roof, and soffit sheathing

60-minute felt paper

Ice and water shield

2 × 6 barn rafters, headers, collar ties

2 × 8 ridge

1 × 4 cedar corner trim

1 × 3 cedar fascia

1 × 6 cedar dentil base molding, door framing, gable end fascia

4 1'6" × 4' gable end windows with obscure glass and operable top awning panel

2 1' × 4' awning-style windows with screens for cupola

1 × 6 tongue-and-groove cedar siding and soffits

2 exterior light fixtures in brushed nickel

Standing-seam galvanized steel roofing, ridge, and edging

Galvanized and stainless-steel nails and screws

Oversized galvanized door hinges and door hardware

2 × 2 and 1 × 2 cedar window framing for cupola and door

Flashing

Tempered glass

Design Details

Build this storage barn on a base of crushed rock and 4-by-4 skids, or install it on a concrete slab or perimeter wall foundation. Check your local building code for requirements (see pages 62–67). Standard 2-by-4 wall framing can be increased to 2 by 6 if the barn's function necessitates insulation. Unique to this structure is the oversized cupola —a separately framed structure with a hip roof built on top of the barn's gable roof. Large, stylized dentil molding anchors the base of the barn, and industrial steel light fixtures, roofing, and door hardware add contrast to the dark gray exterior stain and natural cedar trim. On each gable end, two narrow windows with obscure glass add light while maintaining privacy.

Design by Artisan Sheds. To order plans for this project, see page 190.

continued »

How to Build the Storage Barn

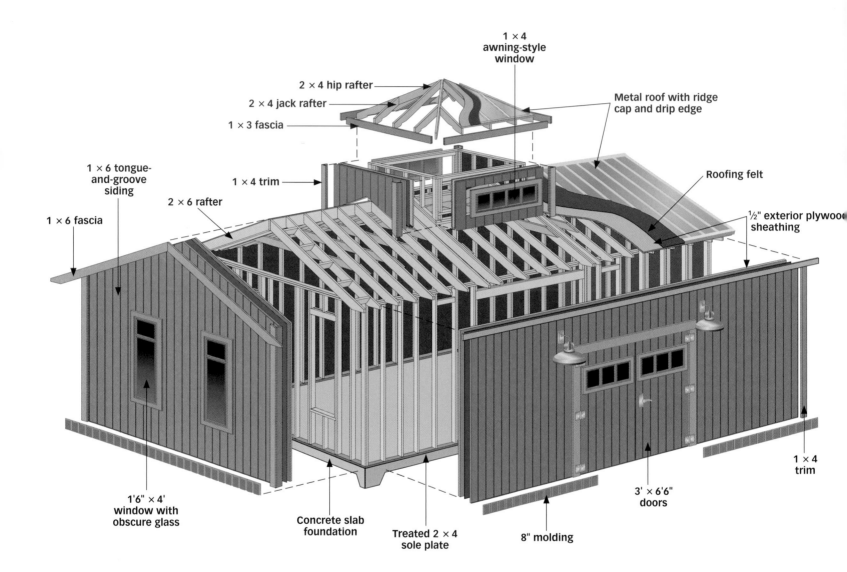

1 × 4 awning-style window

2 × 4 hip rafter

2 × 4 jack rafter

1 × 3 fascia

Metal roof with ridge cap and drip edge

1 × 6 tongue-and-groove siding

1 × 4 trim

2 × 6 rafter

Roofing felt

1 × 6 fascia

½" exterior plywood sheathing

1'6" × 4' window with obscure glass

Concrete slab foundation

Treated 2 × 4 sole plate

8" molding

3' × 6'6" doors

1 × 4 trim

Building Tip: Natural cedar will age to gray unless you seal it frequently with a protective finish.

FRONT DETAIL

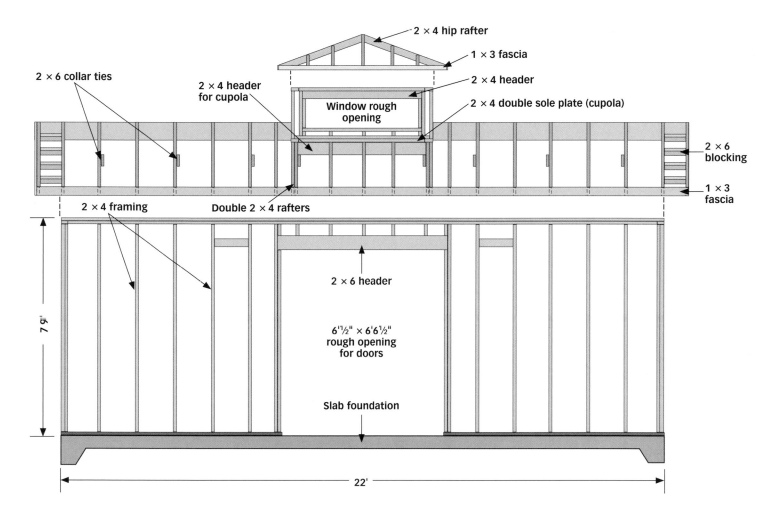

2 × 4 hip rafter

1 × 3 fascia

2 × 6 collar ties

2 × 4 header
for cupola

2 × 4 header

2 × 4 double sole plate (cupola)

Window rough
opening

2 × 6
blocking

1 × 3
fascia

2 × 4 framing

Double 2 × 4 rafters

7 9'

2 × 6 header

6'½" × 6'6½"
rough opening
for doors

Slab foundation

22'

1 INSTALL THE FOUNDATION AND FRAME THE WALLS
Plan for electrical and plumbing needs before constructing the foundation and install essential elements. Lay out, check for square, form, and pour the concrete slab with thickened edge (see pages 66–67). Add reinforcing steel and anchor bolts. After the concrete foundation has cured, frame the walls using a pressure-treated 2 by 4 for the sole plate. Cut the top plates to match and lay out the wall studs 16 inches on center. Frame the rough opening for the entry doors and the gable end windows. Build the walls in sections and add trimmer studs, headers, cripple studs, and sills as required. If you end up with any spacing greater than 16 inches on center, add an extra stud. Install 2-by-4 blocking in the location of the exterior light fixtures.

2 RAISE THE WALLS
Starting with the side walls, place each section over the anchor bolts, add washers and nuts, and hand tighten. Brace each wall panel as necessary. Keep checking for plumb, level, and square. Screw the walls together, install filler blocks, and tighten all connectors. Install the double top plates and mark the corresponding rafter locations.

continued 》

SIDE FRAMING DETAIL

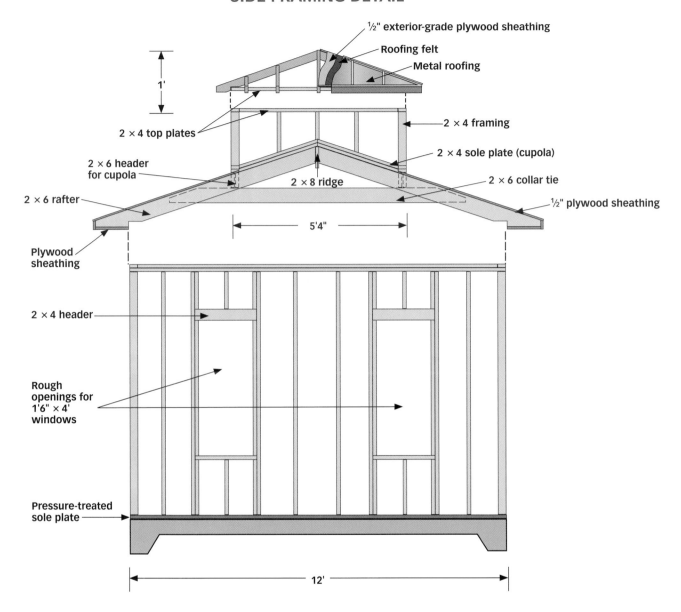

½" exterior-grade plywood sheathing

Roofing felt

Metal roofing

2 × 4 framing

2 × 4 sole plate (cupola)

2 × 4 top plates

2 × 6 header for cupola

2 × 8 ridge

2 × 6 collar tie

2 × 6 rafter

½" plywood sheathing

Plywood sheathing

5'4"

2 × 4 header

Rough openings for 1'6" × 4' windows

Pressure-treated sole plate

12'

3 FRAME THE ROOF Use the same 16-inch-on-center spacing for the rafter locations, but add framing to support the cupola, which is open to the interior below (see roof framing plan). Install the ridge beam with a 1-foot overhang. Using a 4:12 slope, make a rafter template with bird's-mouth cut and 1-foot overhang. The rafter tail will be cut back perpendicular to the walls so that the soffit can be enclosed. Double the rafters that will support the side walls of the cupola but leave out the center rafters where the cupola will be installed. Add 2-by-6 collar ties on the inside of each rafter pair and on alternating rafters. The top of each collar tie is 8 feet 10 inches off the floor slab. Install a double 2-by-6 header with a ½-inch plywood spacer between the doubled rafters and on top of the collar ties. Add partial rafters between the cupola headers and the top sill on both sides of the ridge. Cut the same notch on rafter ends, then install the 1-by-3 fascia. Remove the ridge beam between the two doubled rafters. Build and install a 2-by-6 rake on each gable end and finish with 1-by-6 fascia.

ROOF FRAMING PLAN

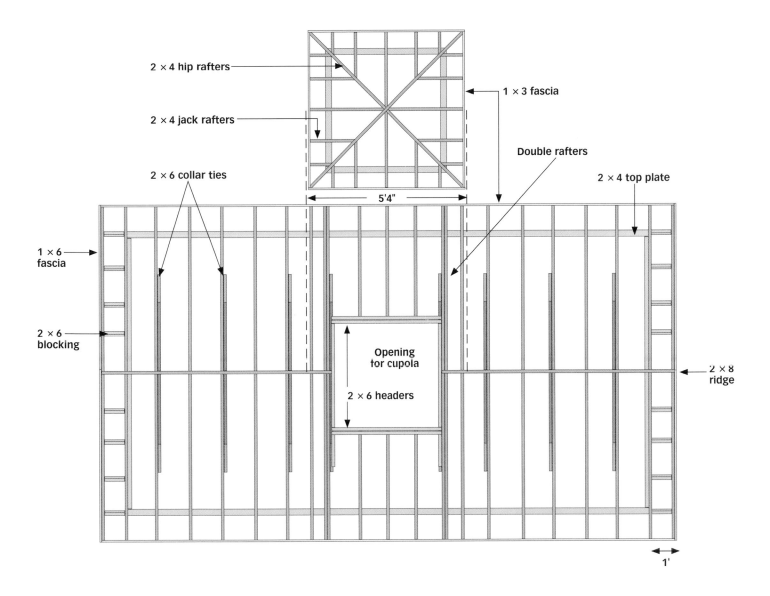

2 × 4 hip rafters

2 × 4 jack rafters

2 × 6 collar ties

1 × 3 fascia

Double rafters

2 × 4 top plate

1 × 6 fascia

2 × 6 blocking

5'4"

Opening for cupola

2 × 6 headers

2 × 8 ridge

1'

4 FRAME THE CUPOLA You will frame the cupola in two sections—the walls and the roof. Frame the wall structure on the ground using the 4:12 roof slope for the side wall sole plates. Frame the rough window openings in the front and back walls. Double-check the fit with the framed roof opening. Secure the walls to each other and add corner filler blocks. Use the top plate as a guide to cut the second top plate, which will be used for framing the roof. Cut 2-by-4 hip rafters with a 4:12 slope and 6-inch overhang. Notch them over the second top plate and cut the rafter tails. Add jack rafters. With help, lift the wall frame into place on the roof framing and secure it. Install the hip roof structure on the top plate and add 1-by-3 fascia to the rafters.

5 INSTALL THE ROOF Sheath the gable roof and the cupola roof with ½-inch exterior plywood. Add a layer of ice and water shield. Install the metal roof following the manufacturer's instructions. Flash all seams between the cupola and the roof. Use both cap or counter flashing and base flashing where the cupola walls meet the roof rafters. Add ridge caps and eave flashing.

continued »

6 INSTALL THE SIDING, WINDOWS, AND TRIM

Sheath the barn and cupola with ½-inch exterior plywood (see pages 80–81). Add a layer of building paper. Install the tongue-and-groove vertical siding. Build the 8-inch base molding from 1-by-8 cedar, beveling the top and sides of each piece and installing the sections in a continuous row on top of the siding. Seal the seam between the siding and trim with silicone caulking. Eliminate the top bevel at each corner where dentil molding meets the 1-by-4 trim. Install the windows per manufacturer's instructions or build custom windows. Add 1-by-4 window trim and 1-by-6 trim around the entry doors. Sheath the underside of the soffits with exterior plywood and trim where the wall and soffit intersect.

7 BUILD AND INSTALL THE DOORS AND FINISH THE INTERIOR

Build the doors with 1-by-6 tongue-and-groove siding and a Z-frame (see page 84). Frame the window openings and build them using pre-cut tempered glass panels and cedar trim pieces. Install the doors, jamb, stop, and hardware. Before adding any interior finishes, make sure that all electrical and plumbing are complete and inspected.

Building Tip: Cupolas, especially if built of wood, take a beating from the weather. Be sure to seal and finish all cut ends, be diligent about flashing, and routinely inspect your cupola for maintenance needs.

MINI BARN

This mini barn, reminiscent of larger traditional-style barns, provides ample storage in a large yard or country setting. Measuring 10 by 12 feet, it's perfect for hard-to-store household items or lawn equipment, and the loft space created by the gambrel roof is a bonus. With the right interior finishes, this barn could easily become a studio or workshop.

Build it on a temporary foundation of skids or blocks, or on a poured slab that doubles as the floor. Gambrel roof trusses are hand built with 2 by 6s and ½-inch plywood gusset plates (see detail), with the 2-by-6 bottom chord creating the floor of the loft. Gusset plates are nailed to each chord using nine 8d nails alternately nailed from the front and back of the truss.

Wall framing is basic 2-by-4 construction. The barn doors are custom-built (see page 84). The roof trusses are covered with plywood sheathing, roofing felt, and asphalt shingles (see page 78). The siding is T1-11 plywood. The entry ramp is ideal for moving equipment in and out.

*Design by HDA, Inc.
To order plans for this project, see page 167.*

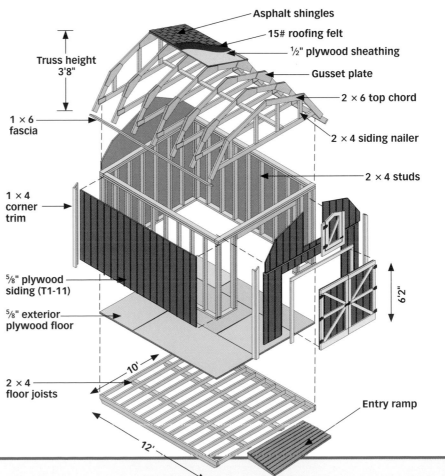

- Asphalt shingles
- 15# roofing felt
- ½" plywood sheathing
- Gusset plate
- 2 × 6 top chord
- 2 × 4 siding nailer
- 2 × 4 studs
- Truss height 3'8"
- 1 × 6 fascia
- 1 × 4 corner trim
- ⅝" plywood siding (T1-11)
- ⅝" exterior plywood floor
- 2 × 4 floor joists
- 6'2"
- 10'
- 12'
- Entry ramp

CLASSIC GABLE BARN

An American classic, this 24-by-30-foot barn with hayloft is large enough to hold livestock, feed, and farm supplies. With five stalls and a feed room, the floor plan is easily adaptable to provide space for a workshop or tack room. The large double doors at each end let you drive through for loading and unloading. Building a barn is a major project. You may want to hire pros to build most or all of the structure and then complete the detailing yourself. The following is a general outline of what's involved. Consider it a resource for basic knowledge and a starting point but know that each barn requires specific engineering calculations based on its size and the type of construction used.

MATERIALS LIST

Framing lumber, concrete, reinforcing steel, wire mesh, anchor bolts—foundation and floor

2 × 4 wall framing, corner bracing

4 × 4 corner posts

Tongue-and-groove flooring

2 × 6 sole plate, roof rafters, loft bracing and collar ties

2 × 10 girder

1 × 6 wall bracing

Horizontal beveled siding

2 × 8 roof ridge

¾" CDX plywood sheathing for roof

60-minute felt paper

Asphalt shingles and ridge

1 × 6 tongue-and-groove and 1 × 6 framing for doors

6 to 8 barn sash windows approximately 2'8" × 3'6" and hardware

2 sets of sliding barn doors 8' wide × 8'6" high

2 sets of sliding barn door track hardware

1 entry door 3'6" × 8'

2 screened wood louvered vents for gable ends

Flashing

Galvanized nails and screws

1 × 6 fascia and trim

Electrical and/or plumbing supplies

Design Details

Built with basic 2-by-4 wall framing and some post-and-beam techniques, this barn is supported by a perimeter wall foundation with footing (see page 63). Two additional foundation walls are constructed down the middle of the structure to support the bearing walls on each side of the driveway. The upper loft floor is framed with 2-by-8 joists and finished with tongue-and-groove flooring. Access the loft through the upper-level exterior door, or frame an opening in the loft floor and add a ladder or a set of stairs. Finish this barn with hand-built doors on sliding barn door tracks, adjustable barn sash windows, horizontal siding, gable end vents, and an asphalt shingle roof. Change the look by opting for a metal roof or alternative siding.

Design by Louisiana State University AgCenter. For more information, see page 190.

continued »

How to Build the Classic Gable Barn

SECTION VIEW

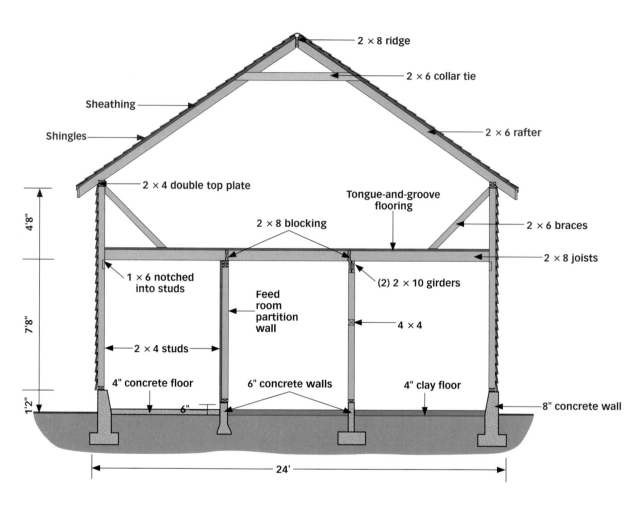

2 × 8 ridge

2 × 6 collar tie

Sheathing

Shingles

2 × 6 rafter

2 × 4 double top plate

Tongue-and-groove flooring

2 × 8 blocking

2 × 6 braces

2 × 8 joists

1 × 6 notched into studs

(2) 2 × 10 girders

4'8"

Feed room partition wall

2 × 4 studs

4 × 4

7'8"

4" concrete floor

6" concrete walls

4" clay floor

1'2"

6"

8" concrete wall

24'

1 FORM AND POUR THE FOUNDATION AND FLOOR
Large perimeter wall foundations are typically handled by professionals. Consider the location of any electrical and plumbing needs before the foundation is poured, and make sure essential elements are in place (see pages 88–89). Form and pour the footings for the perimeter wall and the two intermediate walls using local building codes as your guide for size, depth, and reinforcement. Form and pour the walls on top of the footings with anchor bolts, straps, and door openings in place and add drainage as needed for the footings. The finished foundation wall height is 6 inches above the interior floor level. Reinforce and pour the concrete slab floor between the walls. Depending on function, some interior floors may be clay.

2 FRAME AND RAISE THE FIRST-FLOOR WALLS
Large framing jobs like this are typically built in sections and raised by a crew. Frame the walls for the first floor using 2 by 4s 24 inches on center, a 2-by-4 sill plate and 4-by-4 corner posts (see pages 70–73). The large sliding barn doors on each end are full height, allowing the 2-by-8 joists for the loft floor above to serve as the door headers. Frame the rough openings for the windows and entry door and notch the diagonal bracing into the studs. Frame the partition walls with door and stall openings using double top plates and 2-by-10 girders as shown on the section drawing.

SIDE VIEW

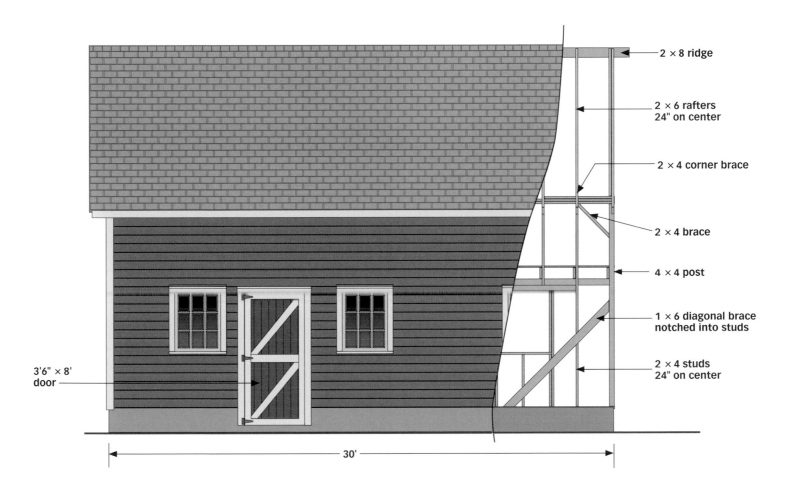

2 × 8 ridge

2 × 6 rafters
24" on center

2 × 4 corner brace

2 × 4 brace

4 × 4 post

1 × 6 diagonal brace
notched into studs

2 × 4 studs
24" on center

3'6" × 8'
door

30'

Building Tip: The easiest way to cut notches for bracing is to make multiple cuts with a circular saw and then clean out the notch with a chisel.

3 FRAME THE LOFT FLOOR AND UPPER WALLS
Frame the loft floor using 2-by-8 joists 24 inches on center. Provide an access opening if desired and install tongue-and-groove flooring. Frame the side and gable end walls, including the gable end vents and the loft door, using 2 by 4s 24 inches on center, a double 2-by-4 top plate and header, and an 8:12 roof pitch. Add 2-by-4 corner bracing to the walls and 2-by-6 braces 6 feet on center extending into the loft (see section and elevation drawings).

continued **»**

FRONT VIEW

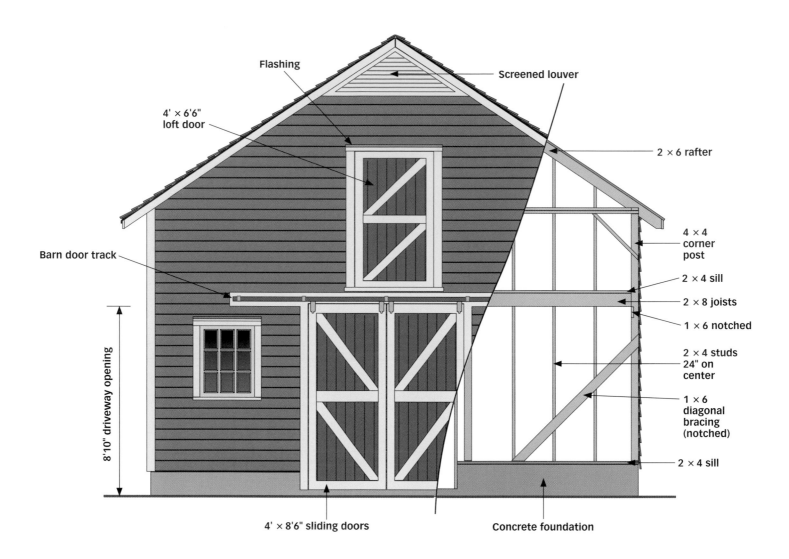

Flashing

Screened louver

4' × 6'6" loft door

2 × 6 rafter

Barn door track

4 × 4 corner post

2 × 4 sill

2 × 8 joists

1 × 6 notched

2 × 4 studs 24" on center

1 × 6 diagonal bracing (notched)

2 × 4 sill

8'10" driveway opening

4' × 8'6" sliding doors

Concrete foundation

4 FRAME AND INSTALL THE ROOF

Set the 2-by-8 ridge with overhang and add the 2-by-6 rafters with bird's-mouth cuts 24 inches on center (see pages 74–77). Install 2-by-6 collar ties on every rafter and build a 1-foot outrigger on the gable ends (see page 75). Add the fascia. Sheath the roof with exterior-grade plywood and roofing felt and install the asphalt shingles with ridge cap. Add necessary flashing (see pages 78–79). Because of this roof's steep slope and height (the ridge is more than 22 feet off the ground), it would be wise to hire professional framers and roofers.

Building Tip: Depending on the location of your barn, you may need to add gutters. Consult a gutter specialist for the number and location of downspouts.

5 ADD TRIM, SIDING, WINDOWS, DOORS, AND VENTS

Install the gable end vents. If you're using beveled siding, add the corner, window and door trim, and a mounting surface for the barn door track before installing the siding and necessary flashing. Install the tilt-in adjustable windows and hardware (see window section). Build the entry door and two sets of sliding barn doors and follow the manufacturer's instructions for adding hardware and roller door guides (see page 84).

6 FINISH THE INTERIOR

Make sure all of the systems—electrical and plumbing—are complete. Finish the box stall partitions and add doors or gates. If you've framed a loft opening in the floor, install stairs or a ladder. Add storage as necessary for feed, supplies, and tools.

Building Tip:

When building horse stalls, add extra space, reinforce the exterior walls, and make windows smaller and higher.

WINDOW DETAIL

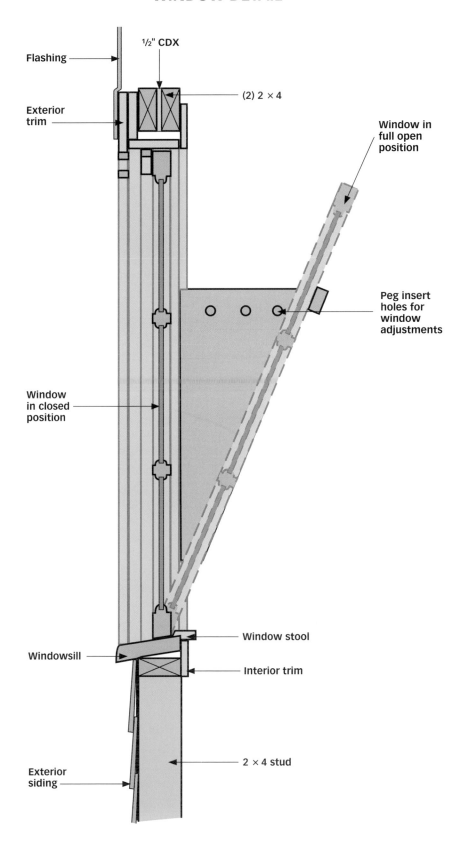

- Flashing
- ½" CDX
- (2) 2 × 4
- Exterior trim
- Window in full open position
- Peg insert holes for window adjustments
- Window in closed position
- Window stool
- Windowsill
- Interior trim
- 2 × 4 stud
- Exterior siding

SHED AND GARAGE PLANS

A new garage or shed can solve your storage problems, provide a protected area for your car and yard equipment, and add charm to your property. If the projects featured earlier in this book aren't quite what you are looking for, or if you need more detailed building plans, then check out the plans for sale on the following pages.

Whether you need a simple shed to house your garden tools, a greenhouse-style shed for the ultimate space to grow your plants and vegetables, a quaint children's playhouse, or even an elaborate garage that extends your living space, you'll find a wide variety of options. And if you build it yourself, you'll have the added satisfaction of watching the structure take shape with each saw cut and every swing of the hammer. The opposite page provides all the ordering information you'll need. Just choose the plan that's right for you from the selection beginning on page 160. If you haven't found the perfect plan, visit project plans.com for many additional shed and garage options. Once you have selected the perfect structure for you and your family, simply call, fax, mail, or order online at project plans.com. You'll be well on your way to an exciting new building project that will enhance your outdoor living and increase your property's value.

Important Information to Know Before You Order

EXCHANGE POLICIES Since blueprints are printed in response to your order, we cannot honor requests for refunds. However, if for some reason you find that the plan you have purchased does not meet your requirements, you may exchange that plan for another plan in our collection within 90 days of purchase. At the time of the exchange, you will be charged a processing fee of 25% of your original plan package price, plus the difference in price between the plan packages (if applicable) and the cost to ship the new plans to you.

Please note: Reproducible drawings can be exchanged only if the package is unopened, and a 25% restocking fee will be charged. PDF and CAD packages are not refundable or returnable.

BUILDING CODES AND REQUIREMENTS At the time the construction drawings were prepared, every effort was made to ensure that the plans and specifications meet nationally recognized codes. Our plans conform to most national building codes. Because building codes vary from area to area, some drawing modifications and/or the assistance of a professional designer or architect may be necessary to comply with your local codes or to accommodate specific building site conditions. We advise you to consult your local building officials for information regarding codes governing your area prior to purchasing a plan.

HOW TO ORDER

For fastest service, call toll-free 1-800-367-7667 day or night

FOUR EASY WAYS TO ORDER

1. CALL toll-free 1-800-367-7667 for credit card orders. MasterCard, Visa, Discover, and American Express are accepted.
2. FAX your order to 1-314-770-2226.
3. MAIL the order form to: HDA, Inc.
   944 Anglum Road
   St. Louis, MO 63042
   Attn: Customer Service Dept.
4. ONLINE visit projectplans.com

QUESTIONS? Call our customer service number: 1-800-367-7667

ORDER FORM

Please send me:

PLAN NUMBER 650-_____

PRICE CODE_____(see above)

CAD package (call for availability) $_____

Reproducible masters (see chart at right) $_____

PDF file (call for availability) $_____

Initial set of plans $_____

Additional plan sets (see chart at right)
_____(Qty) at $_____each

Subtotal $_____

Sales tax (MO residents add 7%) $_____

❑ Shipping/handling (see chart at right) $_____
  (each additional set add $2.00 to
  shipping charges)

TOTAL ENCLOSED (US funds only) $_____

❑ Enclosed is my check or money order payable to HDA, Inc. (Sorry, no CODs)

I hereby authorize HDA, Inc., to charge this purchase to my credit card account (check one):

❑   ❑   ❑   ❑

Credit card number_____

Expiration date_____

Signature_____

Name _____

Street address_____

City _____ (Please print or type)

State_____ Zip _____ (Please do not use PO box)

Daytime phone number (_____)_____

Email address_____

Thank you for your order!

BLUEPRINT PRICE SCHEDULE

Price code	1 set	Additional sets	Reproducible masters/PDF	CAD
P6	$40	$15	$90	$240
P7	$60	$15	$110	$260
P8	$125	$20	$175	$325
P9	$175	$25	$225	$375
P10	$200	$25	$250	$400
P11	$225	$30	$275	$425
P12	$250	$30	$300	$450
P13	$310	$45	$610	$1000

Plan prices are subject to change without notice.
Please note that plan purchases are not refundable.

SHIPPING & HANDLING CHARGES

EACH ADDITIONAL SET ADD $2.00 TO SHIPPING CHARGES

U.S. SHIPPING (AK & HI EXPRESS ONLY)	P6–P7	P8–P13
Regular (allow 7–10 business days)	$10	$15
Priority (allow 3–5 business days)	$15	$35
Express* (allow 1–2 business days)	$25	$50

CANADA SHIPPING**		
Standard (allow 8–12 business days)	$25	$35
Express* (allow 3–5 business days)	$50	$75

OVERSEAS SHIPPING/INTERNATIONAL

Call, fax, or email (plans@hdainc.com) for shipping costs.

  * For express delivery, please call us by 11 a.m. Monday–Friday CST.

** Orders may be subject to custom fees and/or duties/taxes.

Shipping and handling charges do not apply on PDF files. Orders will be emailed within 24 hours (Mon.–Fri. 8–5 CST) of purchase.

Many of our plans are available in CAD and PDF. For availability, please call our customer service number: 1-800-367-7667.

GARDEN SHED

DESIGN #650-002D-4523

Size: 10' × 10'

- Wood floor on 4 × 4 runners
- Height floor to peak: 11'3½"
- Left wall height: 8'
- Wonderful complement to any yard
- Perfect space for lawn equipment or plants and flowers
- Plenty of windows for gardening year-round
- Complete list of materials
- Step-by-step instructions

Price code P7

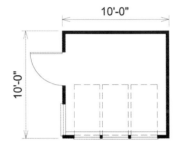

YARD BARNS

DESIGN #650-002D-4502

Sizes: 10' wide × 12' deep
       10' wide × 16' deep
       10' wide × 20' deep

- Wood floor on 4 × 4 runners
- Height floor to peak: 8'4½"
- Ceiling height: 6'4"
- 4' × 6'4" double door for access
- Ample storage area
- Complete list of materials
- Step-by-step instructions

Price code P7

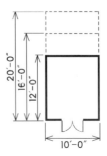

SALTBOX STORAGE SHED

DESIGN #650-002D-4519

Size: 10' wide × 8' deep

- Wood floor on 4 × 4 runners
- Height floor to peak: 9'6"
- Front wall height: 8'
- 4' × 6'8" double door for easy access
- Window adds light to space
- Complete list of materials
- Step-by-step instructions

Price code P7

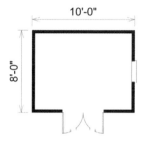

GABLE STORAGE SHEDS

DESIGN #650-002D-4509

Sizes: 8' wide × 8' deep

8' wide × 10' deep

8' wide × 12' deep

- Wood floor on concrete footings
- Height floor to peak: 9'1"
- Wall height: 6'7"
- Circle-top window adds interest and light
- Complete list of materials
- Step-by-step instructions

Price code P6

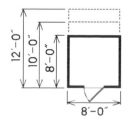

GABLE STORAGE SHED/PLAYHOUSE

DESIGN #650-002D-4522

Size: 12' wide × 8' deep

- Wood floor on 4 × 4 runners
- Height floor to peak: 10'5"
- Ceiling height: 8'
- 3'0" × 6'8" dutch door
- Perfect for storage or playhouse
- Shutters and window box create a charming facade
- Complete list of materials
- Step-by-step instructions

Price code P6

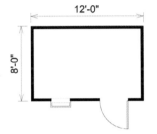

GREENHOUSE

DESIGN #650-002D-4513

Size: 8' wide × 12' deep

- Gravel floor with concrete foundation wall
- Height foundation to peak: 8'3"
- Rear wall height: 7'11"
- An attractive addition to any yard
- Convenient storage for garden tools
- Complete list of materials
- Step-by-step instructions

Price code P7

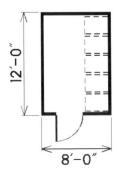

MINI BARN STORAGE SHEDS

DESIGN #650-002D-4510

Sizes: 7'3" wide × 6' deep

7'3" wide × 8' deep

7'3" wide × 10' deep

7'3" wide × 12' deep

- Wood floor on 4 × 6 runners or slab foundation
- Height floor to peak: 9'
- Ceiling height: 7'4"
- 3' × 6'8" door
- Complete list of materials
- Step-by-step instructions

Price code P7

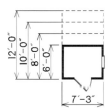

BARN STORAGE SHED WITH OVERHEAD DOOR

DESIGN #650-002D-4521

Size: 12' wide × 16' deep

- Slab foundation
- Height floor to peak: 12'5"
- Ceiling height: 8'
- 8' × 7' overhead door for easy entry with large equipment
- Side windows add light to interior
- Complete list of materials
- Step-by-step instructions

Price code P7

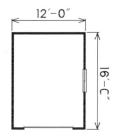

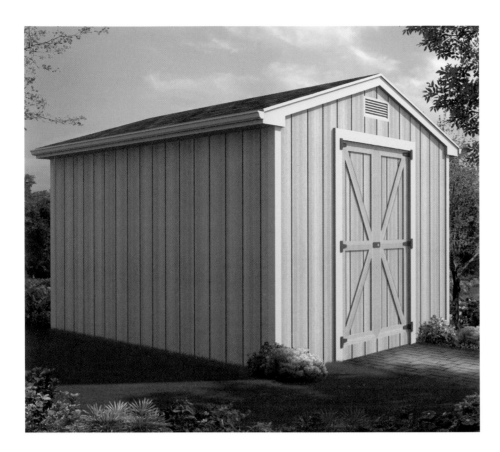

GABLE STORAGE SHEDS

DESIGN #650-002D-4504

Sizes: 10' wide × 12' deep
10' wide × 16' deep
10' wide × 20' deep

• Wood floor on 4 × 4 runners
• Height floor to peak: 8'8½"
• Ceiling height: 7'
• 4' × 6'4" double door for access
• Complete list of materials
• Step-by-step instructions

Price code P7

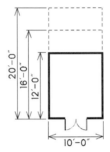

GARDEN SHED

DESIGN #650-002D-4507

Size: 10' wide × 12' deep

• Wood floor on gravel base
• Height floor to peak: 9'9"
• Rear wall height: 7'1½"
• Features skylight windows for optimal plant growth
• Ample room for tool and lawn equipment storage
• Complete list of materials
• Step-by-step instructions

Price code P7

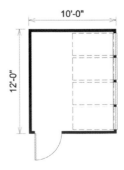

CONVENIENCE SHED

DESIGN #650-002D-4506

Size: 16' wide × 12' deep

- Slab foundation
- Height floor to peak: 12'4½"
- Ceiling height: 8'
- 8' × 7' overhead door
- Ideal for lawn equipment or small-boat storage
- Oversized windows brighten interior
- Complete list of materials
- Step-by-step instructions

Price code P7

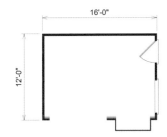

BARN STORAGE SHEDS

DESIGN #650-002D-4508

Sizes: 12' wide × 8' deep

12' wide × 12' deep

12' wide × 16' deep

- Wood floor on pier or slab foundation
- Height floor to peak: 9'10"
- Ceiling height: 7'10"
- 5'6" × 6'8" double door for easy access
- Complete list of materials
- Step-by-step instructions

Price code P7

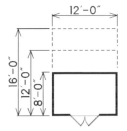

SALTBOX STORAGE SHEDS

DESIGN #650-002D-4500

Sizes: 8' wide × 8' deep

12' wide × 8' deep

16' wide × 8' deep

- Wood floor on gravel base or slab foundation
- Height floor to peak: 8'2"
- Front wall height: 7'
- 6' × 6'5" double door access
- Complete list of materials
- Step-by-step instructions

Price code P7

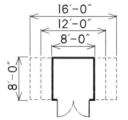

GARDEN SHEDS WITH CLERESTORY

DESIGN #650-002D-4515

Sizes: 10' wide × 10' deep

12' wide × 10' deep

14' wide × 10' deep

- Wood floor on 4 × 6 runners
- Height floor to peak: 10'11"
- Rear wall height: 7'3"
- Clerestory windows for added light
- Complete list of materials
- Step-by-step instructions

Price code P7

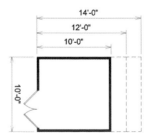

YARD BARN WITH LOFT STORAGE

DESIGN #650-002D-4520

Size: 10' wide × 12' deep

- Wood floor on 4 × 4 runners
- Height floor to peak: 10'7"
- Ceiling height: 6'11"
- 6' × 6'2" double door for easy access
- Loft provides additional storage area
- Attractive styling is suitable for any yard
- Complete list of materials
- Step-by-step instructions

Price code P7

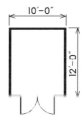

MINI BARNS

DESIGN #650-002D-4524

Sizes: 8' wide × 8' deep
      8' wide × 10' deep
      8' wide × 12' deep
      8' wide × 16' deep

- Wood floor on 4 × 4 runners
- Height floor to peak: 7'6"
- Ceiling height: 6'
- 4' × 6' double door for easy access
- Attractive styling for any backyard
- Complete list of materials
- Step-by-step instructions

Price code P7

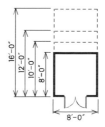

STORAGE SHED WITH PLAYHOUSE LOFT

DESIGN #650-002D-4514

Size: 12' × 12' with 2'8" balcony

- Wood floor on pier or slab foundation
- Height floor to peak: 14'1"
- Ceiling height: 7'4"
- 4' × 6'10" door
- Loft with ladder can be used as playhouse for children
- Complete list of materials
- Step-by-step instructions

Price code P6

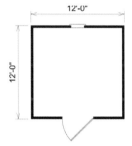

CHILDREN'S PLAYHOUSE

DESIGN #650-002D-4505

Size: 8' wide × 8' deep

- Wood floor on 4 × 4 runners
- Height floor to peak: 9'2"
- Ceiling height: 6'1"
- 2' deep porch
- Attractive window boxes
- Includes operable windows
- Complete list of materials
- Step-by-step instructions

Price code P6

GABLE STORAGE SHEDS

DESIGN #650-002D-4503

Sizes: 8' wide × 8' deep

8' wide × 10' deep

8' wide × 12' deep

8' wide × 16' deep

- Wood floor on 4 × 4 runners
- Height floor to peak: 8'4½"
- Ceiling height: 6'9.5"
- Complete list of materials
- Step-by-step instructions

Price code P7

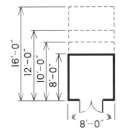

CHILDREN'S PLAYHOUSE

DESIGN #650-002D-4517

Size: 6' wide × 6' deep

- Wood floor on gravel base
- Height floor to peak: 7'2"
- Wall height: 4'4"
- Plenty of openings brighten interior
- Gabled doorway and window box add interest
- Complete list of materials
- Step-by-step instructions

Price code P6

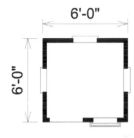

MULTIPURPOSE BARN

DESIGN #650-002D-7501

Size: 24' wide × 36' deep

- Floating slab foundation
- Building height: 23'8"
- Ceiling heights: First floor 9'
                    Loft 9'9"
- Roof pitches: 4:12, 12:4
- Two 9' × 9' sliding doors
- Loft designed for 100 p.s.f. live load
- Complete list of materials
- Step-by-step instructions

Price code P12

I-CAR GARAGE WITH COVERED PORCH

DESIGN #650-002D-6010

Size: 24' wide × 22' deep

- Building height: 13'
- Roof pitch: 5:12
- Ceiling height: 8'
- 9' × 7' overhead door
- Floating slab foundation; drawings also include slab foundation
- Distinctive covered porch area
- Complete list of materials
- Step-by-step instructions

Price code P9

BARN STORAGE SHEDS WITH LOFT

DESIGN #650-002D-4501

Sizes: 12' wide × 12' deep
        12' wide × 16' deep
        12' wide × 20' deep

- Wood floor on pier or slab foundation
- Height floor to peak: 12'10"
- Ceiling height: 7'4"
- 4' × 6'8" double door for easy access
- Complete list of materials
- Step-by-step instructions

Price code P7

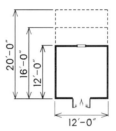

POLE BUILDING: HORSE BARN WITH LOFT

DESIGN #650-002D-7511

Size: 26' wide × 48' deep

- Compacted clay floor in stalls, concrete slab floor
- Building height: 22'
- Ceiling heights: First floor 9'
                    Loft 11'
- Roof pitch: 6:12
- Loft designed for 75 p.s.f. live load
- Complete list of materials
- Step-by-step instructions

Price code P12

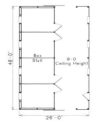

WORKROOM WITH COVERED PORCH

DESIGN #650-002D-7520

Size: 24' wide × 20' deep

- Building height: 13'6"
- Roof pitch: 6:12
- Ceiling height: 8'
- Slab foundation
- Easy access with double door entry
- Interior enhanced by large windows
- Complete list of materials
- Step-by-step instructions

Price code P9

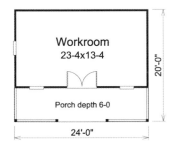

Workroom
23-4x13-4

20'-0"

Porch depth 6-0

24'-0"

2-CAR GARAGE: VICTORIAN STYLE

DESIGN #650-002D-6018

Size: 24' wide × 24' deep

- Building height: 16'7"
- Roof pitch: 8:12
- Ceiling height: 8'
- Two 9' × 7' overhead doors
- Floating slab foundation; drawings also include slab foundation
- Functional side entry
- Complete list of materials
- Step-by-step instructions

Price code P10

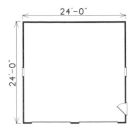

24'-0"

24'-0"

1-CAR GARAGE WESTERN STYLE

DESIGN #650-002D-6022

Size: 14' wide × 22' deep

- Building height: 10'10"
- Roof pitch: 4:12
- Ceiling height: 8'
- 9' × 7' overhead door
- Floating slab foundation; drawings also include slab foundation
- Compact size perfect for small lots
- Complete list of materials
- Step-by-step instructions

Price code P8

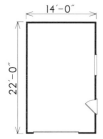

2-CAR GARAGE WITH 8' HIGH DOOR

DESIGN #650-002D-6019

Size: 24' wide × 26' deep

- Building height: 13'8"
- Roof pitch: 4:12
- Ceiling height: 9'
- 16' × 8' overhead door
- Floating slab foundation; drawings also include slab foundation
- Side window adds light
- Complete list of materials
- Step-by-step instructions

Price code P10

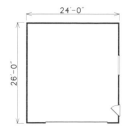

2½-CAR GARAGE: WESTERN STYLE

DESIGN #650-002D-6024

Size: 30' wide × 24' deep

- Building height: 12'6"
- Roof pitch: 4:12
- Ceiling height: 8'
- Two 9' × 7' overhead doors
- Floating slab foundation; drawings also include slab foundation
- Plenty of space is great for storage or workshop
- Complete list of materials
- Step-by-step instructions

Price code P11

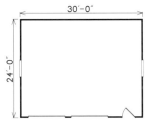

1-CAR GARAGES

DESIGN #650-002D-6028

Sizes: 14' wide × 22' deep
      14' wide × 24' deep
      16' wide × 22' deep
      16' wide × 24' deep

- Building height: 11'2"
- Roof pitch: 4:12
- Ceiling height: 8'
- 9' × 7' overhead door
- Floating slab foundation; drawings also include slab foundation
- Complete list of materials
- Step-by-step instructions

Price code P8

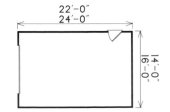

2-CAR ECONOMY GARAGE

DESIGN #650-002D-6032

Size: 20' wide × 20' deep

- Building height: 11'10"
- Roof pitch: 4:12
- Ceiling height: 8'
- 16' × 7' overhead door
- Floating slab foundation; drawings also include slab foundation
- Convenient side door
- Complete list of materials
- Step-by-step instructions

Price code P10

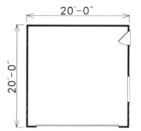

2-CAR GARAGE

DESIGN #650-002D-6013

Size: 22' wide × 22' deep

- Building height: 12'2"
- Roof pitch: 4:12
- Ceiling height: 8'
- 16' × 7' overhead door
- Floating slab foundation; drawings also include slab foundation
- Convenient side entry door
- Complete list of materials
- Step-by-step instructions

Price code P11

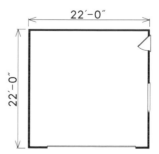

2-CAR GARAGE WITH LOFT

DESIGN #650-002D-6001

Size: 28' wide × 24' deep

- Building height: 21'
- Roof pitch: 12:12
- Ceiling heights: First floor 8'
  Loft 7'6"
- Two 9' × 7' overhead doors
- Floating slab foundation; drawings also include slab foundation
- Complete list of materials
- Step-by-step instructions

Price code P11

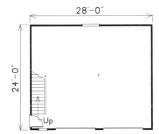

2-CAR GARAGE: GAMBREL ROOF

DESIGN #650-002D-6031

Size: 24' wide × 24' deep

- Building height: 15'5"
- Roof pitch: 4:12
- Ceiling height: 8'
- 16' × 7' overhead door
- Floating slab foundation; drawings also include slab foundation
- Attractive addition to any home
- Complete list of materials
- Step-by-step instructions

Price code P10

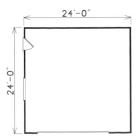

2-CAR GARAGE: ATTACHED OR DETACHED

DESIGN #650-002D-6030

Size: 22' wide × 24' deep
- Building height: 12'8"
- Roof pitch: 4:12
- Ceiling height: 8'
- 16' × 7' overhead door
- Floating slab foundation; drawings also include slab foundation
- Convenient service front door
- Complete list of materials
- Step-by-step instructions

Price code P10

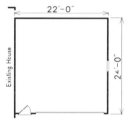

2-CAR GARAGE: REVERSE GABLE

DESIGN #650-002D-6027

Size: 24' wide × 24' deep
- Building height: 16'7"
- Roof pitch: 8:12
- Ceiling height: 8'
- Two 9' × 7' overhead doors
- Floating slab foundation; drawings also include slab foundation
- Easy, functional design
- Complete list of materials
- Step-by-step instructions

Price code P10

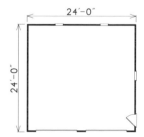

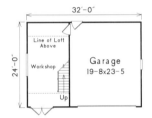

2-CAR GARAGE WITH WORKSHOP AND PARTIAL LOFT

DESIGN #650-002D-6002

Size: 32' wide × 24' deep

- Building height: 20'2"
- Roof pitch: 10:12
- Ceiling heights: First floor 9'8"
                           Loft 8'
- 16' × 7' overhead door
- Floating slab foundation
- Convenient loft above workshop
- Complete list of materials
- Step-by-step instructions

Price code P12

3-CAR GARAGE

DESIGN #650-002D-6046

Size: 40' wide × 24' deep

- Building height: 15'6"
- Roof pitch: 6:12
- Ceiling height: 9'
- Three 9' × 7' overhead doors
- Floating slab foundation; drawings also include slab foundation
- Oversized with room for storage
- Side door for easy access
- Complete list of materials
- Step-by-step instructions

Price code P12

3-CAR GARAGE WITH WORKSHOP

DESIGN #650-002D-6020

Size: 32' wide × 28' deep

- Building height: 13'3"
- Roof pitch: 4:12
- Ceiling height: 8'
- 9' × 7' and 16' × 7' overhead doors
- Floating slab foundation; drawings also include slab foundation
- Handy workshop space for hobbies
- Side entry door for easy access
- Complete list of materials
- Step-by-step instructions

Price code P12

I-CAR GARAGE

DESIGN #650-002D-6005

Size: 14' wide × 22' deep

- Building height: 10'10"
- Roof pitch: 4:12
- Ceiling height: 8'
- 9' × 7' overhead door
- Floating slab foundation; drawings also include slab foundation
- Side window enhances exterior
- Side entry is convenient
- Complete list of materials
- Step-by-step instructions

Price code P8

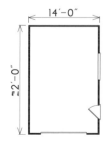

2-CAR CARPORT WITH STORAGE

DESIGN #650-002D-6045

Size: 24' wide × 24' deep

- Building height: 12'8"
- Roof pitch: 4:12
- Ceiling height: 8'
- Slab foundation
- Unique design allows cars to enter from the front or the side of carport
- Deep storage space for large items
- Complete list of materials
- Step-by-step instructions

Price code P9

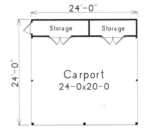

3-CAR GARAGE

DESIGN #650-002D-6025

Size: 30' wide × 24' deep

- Building height: 13'8"
- Roof pitch: 5:12
- Ceiling height: 8'
- 16' × 7' and 9' × 7' overhead doors
- Floating slab foundation; drawings also include slab foundation
- Functional design with side door
- Complete list of materials
- Step-by-step instructions

Price code P12

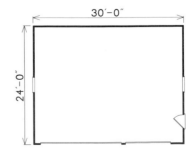

3-CAR GARAGE WITH LOFT

DESIGN #650-002D-6044

Size: 36' wide × 24' deep

- Building height: 20'8"
- Roof pitch: 12:12
- Ceiling heights: First floor 8'
  Loft 7'6"
- Three 9' × 7' overhead doors
- Floating slab foundation
- Third stall is perfect for boat storage
- Generous loft space
- Complete list of materials
- Step-by-step instructions

Price code P12

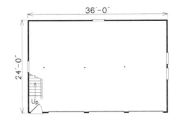

1-CAR GARAGE WITH LOFT: GAMBREL ROOF

DESIGN #650-002D-6043

Size: 16' wide × 24' deep

- Building height: 18'9"
- Roof pitches: 6:12
- Ceiling heights: First floor 8'
  Loft 6'7"
- 9' × 7' overhead door
- Floating slab foundation
- Ideal loft perfect for workshop or storage area
- Complete list of materials
- Step-by-step instructions

Price code P9

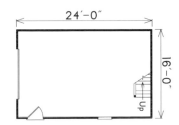

2-CAR GARAGE WITH WORKSHOP AND LOFT

DESIGN #650-002D-6004

Size: 32' wide × 24' deep

- Building height: 21'
- Roof pitch: 12:12
- Ceiling heights: First floor 8'
                   Loft 7'6"
- Two 9' × 7' overhead doors
- Floating slab foundation; drawings also include slab foundation
- Complete list of materials
- Step-by-step instructions

Price code P12

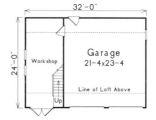

3-CAR GARAGE WITH LOFT: WESTERN STYLE

DESIGN #650-002D-6026

Size: 32' wide × 24' deep

- Building height: 20'6"
- Roof pitch: 12:12
- Ceiling height: 8'
- 9' × 7' and 16' × 7' overhead doors
- Floating slab foundation; drawings also include slab foundation
- Large side windows draw in light
- Complete list of materials
- Step-by-step instructions

Price code P12

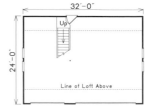

3-CAR GARAGE: WORKSHOP

DESIGN #650-002D-6042

Size: 24' wide × 36' deep

- Building height: 14'6"
- Roof pitch: 4:12
- Ceiling height: 10'
- Three 9' × 8' overhead doors
- Floating slab foundation; drawings also include slab foundation
- Oversized for storage, workshop, or maintenance building
- Complete list of materials
- Step-by-step instructions

Price code P12

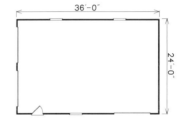

2-CAR GARAGE WITH LOFT

DESIGN #650-002D-6039

Size: 28' wide × 24' deep

- Building height: 21'
- Roof pitch: 12:12
- Ceiling heights: First floor 8'
                    Loft 7'6"
- Two 9' × 7' overhead doors
- Floating slab foundation
- Charming dormers add character
- Handy side door accesses stairs to loft
- Complete list of materials

Price code P11

2-CAR GARAGE WITH LOFT

DESIGN #650-002D-6015

Size: 26' wide × 24' deep

- Building height: 20'
- Roof pitch: 6:12
- Ceiling height: 8'
- Two 9' × 7' overhead doors
- Floating slab foundation
- Loft provides extra space, and clerestory windows brighten the interior
- Complete list of materials
- Step-by-step instructions

Price code P11

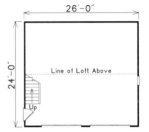

2½-CAR GARAGE

DESIGN #650-002D-6007

Size: 30' wide × 22' deep

- Building height: 12'2"
- Roof pitch: 4:12
- Ceiling height: 8'
- 16' × 7' overhead door
- Floating slab foundation; drawings also include slab foundation
- Additional space is perfect for yard equipment storage
- Complete list of materials
- Step-by-step instructions

Price code P10

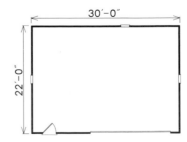

2-CAR GARAGE WITH LOFT: GAMBREL ROOF

DESIGN #650-002D-6000

Size: 22' wide × 26' deep

- Building height: 20'7"
- Roof pitch: 7:12
- Ceiling heights: First floor 8'
                    Loft 7'4"
- Two 9' × 7' overhead doors
- Floating slab foundation
- Complete list of materials
- Step-by-step instructions

Price code P11

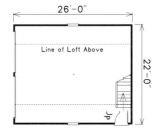

SHOP & EQUIPMENT GARAGE

DESIGN #650-009D-7518

Size: 80' wide × 32' deep

- Building height: 21'
- Roof pitch: 6:12
- Ceiling heights: Shop 10'
                    Garage 12'
- Five 12' × 10' and one 12' × 8' overhead doors
- Slab foundation
- 613 square feet of finished space in the shop
- Complete list of materials

Price code P12

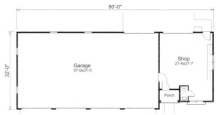

3-CAR GARAGE APARTMENT

DESIGN #650-002D-7529

Size: 40' wide × 26' deep

- 1,040 square feet of living area on the second floor
- Building height: 23'
- Roof pitch: 5:12
- Ceiling heights: First floor 8'
  Second floor 8'
- Three 9' × 7' overhead doors
- 2 bedrooms, 1 bath
- Floating slab foundation
- Large rooms offer comfortable living with second-floor laundry, ample cabinets, and sliding doors to deck
- Complete list of materials

Price code P13

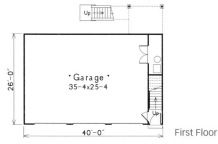

First Floor

Second Floor

2-CAR GARAGE APARTMENT

DESIGN #650-009D-7502

Size: 28' wide × 26' deep

- 632 square feet of living area
- Building height: 26'6"
- Roof pitches: 8:12, 9:12
- Ceiling heights   First floor 9'
  Second floor 8'
- 16' × 7' overhead door
- 1 bedroom, 1 bath
- Floating slab foundation
- Cozy living room offers vaulted ceiling, fireplace, and a pass-through kitchen
- Complete list of materials

Price code P13

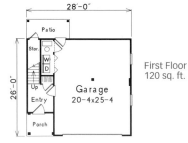

First Floor
120 sq. ft.

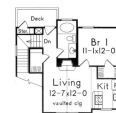

Second Floor
512 sq. ft.

COMFORTABLE COTTAGE

DESIGN #650-009D-7532

Size: 27' wide × 27' deep

- 421 square feet of living area
- Building height: 15'6"
- Roof pitch: 6:12
- Ceiling height: 8'
- 9' × 7' overhead door
- 1 bedroom, 1 bath
- Slab foundation
- The exterior, with its compact plan and recessed entry, has a warm and cozy feel
- Cottage consists of a living room with large bay window and convenient kitchenette, bedroom with bath and closet
- Complete list of materials

Price code P13

3-CAR GARAGE WITH REAR APARTMENT

DESIGN #650-009D-7509

Size: 40' wide × 38' deep

- 1,005 square feet of living area
- Building height: 25'
- Roof pitches: 3.5:12, 6:12, 8:12
- Ceiling heights: First floor 9'
                    Second floor 8'
- Three 9' × 8' overhead doors
- 2 bedrooms, 1½ baths
- Floating slab foundation; drawings also include slab foundation
- Two-story apartment is disguised with one-story facade featuring triple garage doors and roof dormer
- Complete list of materials

Price code P13

First Floor
513 sq. ft.

Second Floor
492 sq. ft.

Second Floor
495 sq. ft.

First Floor
591 sq. ft.

2-CAR APARTMENT GARAGE WITH STYLE

DESIGN #650-009D-7535

Size: 32'8" wide × 39'4" deep

- 1,086 square feet of living area
- Building height: 21'6"
- Roof pitches: 3:12, 5:12
- Ceiling heights: First floor 8'
  Second floor 8'
- Two 9' × 7' overhead doors
- 1 bedroom, 1½ baths
- Slab foundation
- Open to the living room, the U-shaped kitchen has a snack bar and adjacent laundry area with large storage pantry
- Double doors, clerestory roof and a columned porch all add a sense of charm and class
- Complete list of materials

Price code P13

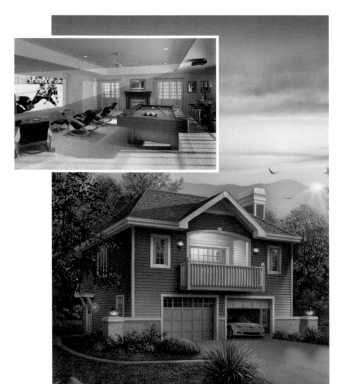

Second Floor
960 sq. ft.

First Floor
210 sq. ft.

HOME SPORTS BAR WITH THEATER

DESIGN #650-009D-7522

Size: 34' wide × 32' deep

- 1,170 square feet of living area
- Building height: 25'6"
- Roof pitches: 5:12, 8:12
- Ceiling heights: First floor 8'
  Second floor 8'
- Two 10' × 7' overhead doors
- Slab foundation
- The first floor consists of a 2-car garage with shop, office, storage, and mechanical closets
- The second floor features a movie theater with 10' screen, fireplace, wet bar, bath, three closets, and a separate entry
- Complete list of materials

Price code P13

Second Floor
566 sq. ft.

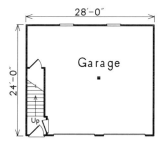

First Floor

2-CAR GARAGE APARTMENT: CAPE COD

DESIGN #650-002D-7526

Size: 28' wide × 24' deep

- 566 square feet of living area
- Building height: 22'
- Roof pitches: 4.5:12, 12:12
- Ceiling heights: First floor 8'
  Second floor 7'7"
- Two 9' × 7' overhead doors
- Studio with bath
- Floating slab foundation
- Charming dormers add appeal to this design
- Comfortable open living area
- Complete list of materials
- Step-by-step instructions

Price code P13

Second Floor
746 sq. ft.

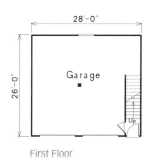

First Floor

2-CAR GARAGE APARTMENT WITH INTERIOR ENTRANCE

DESIGN #650-002D-7510

Size: 28' wide × 26' deep

- 746 square feet of living area
- Building height: 22'
- Roof pitch: 4:12
- Ceiling height: 8'
- Two 9' × 7' overhead doors
- 1 bedroom, 1 bath
- Floating slab foundation
- Complete list of materials
- Step-by-step instructions

Price code P13

Resource Guide

The following organizations, manufacturers, and retail sources will be helpful in designing and constructing your new shed, garage, or barn. Whenever possible, you are encouraged to patronize suppliers in your community and those dedicated to environmentally responsible manufacturing processes and products. To find a local supplier, check online sources listed here for dealers in your ZIP code or look in the Yellow Pages under these headings: Building Materials, Hardware, Lumberyard and Masonry Supplies.

Featured Projects

Artisan Sheds
716-337-3550
www.artisansheds.com
Cupola Shed (page 120); Storage Barn (page 144)

Bob Bowling Rustics
360-331-2528
bobbowlingrustics.homestead.com
Garden Storage Shed (page 111)

Cedarshed Industries
800-830-8033
www.cedarshed.com
Utility Shed (page 98); Garden Hutch (page 102) and Recycling Center (page 103); Hobby Greenhouse (page 137)

HDA, Inc.
800-367-7667
www.houseplansandmore.com
Playhouse with Front Porch and Shutters (page 119); Greenhouse Shed (page 130); Mini Barn (page 151)

Jamaica Cottage Shop
866-297-3760
www.jamaicacottageshop.com
Saltbox Shed (page 104); Saltbox Shed with Wood Storage (page 110); 6-by-8 Greenhouse (page 136)

Jean Zaputil Garden Design
206-755-9832
www.jeanzaputil.com
Hip Roof Shed (page 112); Chicken Coop (page 118); Garden Shed with Architectural Salvage (page 121); Craftsman Garage (page 138); French Door Garage (page 143)

Louisiana State University AgCenter
225-578-3153
www.lsuagcenter.com
Classic Gable Barn (page 152)

NeoShed
240-527-4517
www.neoshed.com
Butterfly Roof Shed (page 122)

Studio Shed
888-900-3933
www.studio-shed.com
Backyard Studio (pages 128–129)

Manufacturers, Prefabricated Structures, Modular Structures, Kits, and Building Plans

Better Barns
888-266-1960
www.betterbarns.com

Better Built Barns Inc.
800-941-2417
www.betterbuiltbarns.com

Garages, Etc.
800-287-3910
www.garagesetc.com

The Garlinghouse Co.
800-235-5700
www.garlinghouse.com

Groffdale Barns
717-687-8350
www.groffdalebarns.com

Kithaus
310-889-7137
www.kithaus.com

Modern Cabana
415-206-9330
www.moderncabana.com

Modern-Shed
800-261-7282
www.modern-shed.com

Pine Harbor Wood Products
800-368-7433
www.pineharbor.com

Summerwood Products
866-519-4634
www.summerwood.com

Walpole Woodworkers
800-343-6948
www.walpolewoodworkers.com

Wooden Shed Kits
800-590-2508
www.woodenshedkits.com

Tools, Materials, and Supplies

Green Depot
www.greendepot.com

The Home Depot
www.homedepot.com

Lowe's
www.lowes.com

Mutual Materials
800-477-3008
www.mutualmaterials.com

True Value
www.truevalue.com

Architectural Salvage and Recycled Materials

Reusable building materials exchanges are often administered by local municipal or county governments as a clearinghouse for free or inexpensive recycled materials. Search "reusable building materials" for a program near you.

Re-Store
www.re-store.org

Index

Credits

PHOTOGRAPHERS

Ableimages/Photodisc/Getty Images: 2L, 6; **Scott Atkinson:** 38TR, 43BL, 54BL, 54BRC, 54BR; **courtesy of Bonded Logic:** 54BLC; **Kira Brandt/Pure Public/Living Inside:** 20 (styling: Katrine Martensen-Larsen); **Comstock Images/Getty Images:** 2 right, 36; **Steve Cory:** 38BR; **Scott Fitzgerrell:** 38TL, 38BL, 38BM, 40TR #1, 40TR #2, 40BL, 40BML, 40BMR, 47 #5, 47 #7, 92; **Jonathan Gelber/Getty Images:** 3C, 96; **Tria Giovan:** front cover bottom #2, 10, 25B, 33; **Glow Images, Inc./Getty Images:** 3R; **John Granen:** 5; **Jamie Hadley:** front cover bottom #3 (design: Gary Tintle/Tintle, Inc.), 39ML, 39MC, 39MR, 39BL, 40MR, 40BR, 43TR, 43BR, 45 both, 46TL, 47 #6, 48 all, 49TR, 49MR, 50 all, 51 top, 52 both, 53L, 55BL, 55TR, 64 all, 68, 69 all, 72L, 80, 84 both, 91BL, 91BR, 95 all; **Jerry Harpur/Harpur Garden Images:** 26B; **Marcus Harpur/Harpur Garden Images:** 27; **HDA, Inc.:** 28B, 119, 151, 158–189; **Saxon Holt:** 8; **Huntstock/Getty Images:** 3L, 56; **Image Source/Getty Images:** 41; **Dency Kane:** 23, 26T; **Fiona Lea/Gap Photos:** 21; **Chris Leschinsky:** 35; **Jason Liske:** 34; **Living Inside:** 28T; **MMGI/Marianne Majerus:** 15B, 32; **Stephanie Massey/Susan A. Roth & Company:** 31T; **Steven Miric/Getty Images:** 17; **courtesy of Modern-Shed:** 9B, 14 (photography by Chad Holder); **Olson Photographic, LLC:** front cover top; **Norman A. Plate:** 44, 46ML, 46MC, 46MR, 46BL, 46BM, 46BR, 47 #8–#10; **courtesy of**

Robert Bosch Tool Corporation: 39TR; **Eric Roth:** front cover bottom #1, 1, 11, 12, 13B, 19, 24, 53R, 58; **Susan A. Roth:** 9T, 16, 18, 22T, 29, 51B; **Mark Rutherford:** 40TL, 42TM, 42TR, 42BL; **David Schiff:** 39TL, 39BR, 40ML; **Jason Smalley/Gap Photos:** 22B; **Tim Street-Porter:** 30; **Studio Shed:** 128, 129 both; **E. Spencer Toy:** 42TL, 42ML, 42BR, 43TL, 47 #1–#4, 47 #11, 47 #12, 55MR; **Mark Turner:** front cover bottom #4, 13T, 25T, 31B; **Christopher Vendetta:** 49TL, 49BR, 65 all, 66 both, 67 all, 71 all, 72M, 72R, 73 both, 76 all, 77 all, 78 all, 79 all, 81, 82, 83, 85 all, 86 all, 87 both, 90, 91TL, 91TML, 91TMR, 91TR, 93 all, back cover top, back cover bottom; **Juliette Wade/Gap Photos:** 15 top; **Jean Zaputil:** 118

DESIGNERS

Artisan Sheds: 120T, 145; **www.benjamin nutter.com:** 53R; **Bob Bowling Rustics:** 111T; **George Carter:** 27; **Cedarshed:** 99, 102T, 103T, 137T; **Mark Gregory** (The Children's Society Garden, Chelsea Flower Show 2008): 15B; **www.deckhouse.com:** 11; **HDA, Inc.:** 119, 131, 151; **Jamaica Cottage Shop:** 105, 110T, 136TR; **Louisiana State University AgCenter:** 153; **Ulf Nordfjell:** 26B; **Paula Manchester:** 9T, 16; **NeoShed:** 123; **Tom Pellett:** 18; **Barbara Robinson:** 22T; **Teresa Scholly and John Holt:** 29; **Claudia Scholz:** 51B; **www.spacecraftarch. com:** 12; **Studio Shed:** 128, 129 both; **Tony**

Wagstaff (The Home Front, RHS Hampton Court Flower Show 2011): 32; **Jean Zaputil:** 113, 118, 121, 139, 143T

ILLUSTRATORS

Troy Doolittle: 59 both, 60, 61 both, 62 both, 63 all, 74 both, 75 all, 88, 89, 94 both; **Bill Oetinger:** 68T, 70, 80L, 81R, 82L, 83R, 84L, 87BR, 90L, 92L, 95T; **Ian Worpole:** 99, 100 both, 101, 102 both, 103 both, 105, 106, 107 both, 108, 109, 110 both, 111 both, 113, 114, 115, 116, 117, 118B, 119B, 120 both, 121, 123, 124, 125, 126 both, 131, 132, 133, 134, 135, 136 all, 137 both, 139, 140, 141 both, 143 both, 145, 146, 147, 148, 149, 151B, 153, 154, 155, 156, 157, back cover middle

SPECIAL THANKS

Mark Hawkins, Charla Lawhon, Haley Minick, Marisa Park, Marie Pence, Alan Phinney, Lorraine Reno, Margaret Sloan, Tony Soria, Vanessa Speckman, Katie Tamony, E. Spencer Toy